A Wooden Spoon
Baking Memoir

BOOKS BY MARILYN M. MOORE

A Wooden Spoon Baking Memoir

The Wooden Spoon Book of Old Family Recipes
(previously titled *Meat and Potatoes and Other Comfort Foods
from The Wooden Spoon Kitchen*)

The Self-Published Cook

The Wooden Spoon Cookie Book

*The Wooden Spoon Book of Home-Style Soups,
Stews, Chowders, Chilis and Gumbos*

The Wooden Spoon Dessert Book

The Wooden Spoon Bread Book

Baking Your Own

A Wooden Spoon
Baking Memoir

Apple-Butter Muffins, Shoofly Pie, and

Other Amish-Mennonite Favorites

Marilyn M. Moore

Atlantic Monthly Press

NEW YORK

Published simultaneously in Canada
Printed in the United States of America
FIRST EDITION

Library of Congress Cataloging-in-Publication Data
Moore, Marilyn M.
    A wooden spoon baking memoir : apple-butter muffins, shoofly pie,
and other Amish-Mennonite favorites / Marilyn M. Moore.
    — 1st ed.
        p.   cm.
    Includes index.
    ISBN 0-87113-700-3
    1. Baking.   2. Cookery, Mennonite.   I. Title.
TX763.M59   1997
641.8'65—dc21   96-47069

DESIGN BY LAURA HAMMOND HOUGH

Atlantic Monthly Press
841 Broadway
New York, NY 10003

10 9 8 7 6 5 4 3 2 1

In memory of my grandmothers—
MARIA WALL JANZEN (BORN 1866, RUSSIA)
HELENA LOEWEN NACHTIGAL (BORN 1873, RUSSIA)

Contents

Our Daily Bread 85

Plain and Simple Rolls 97

Quick Bakery Breads and Coffee Cakes 107

Standard Preparations 125

Bibliography 131

Index 133

Introduction

This is a book I have wanted to write for a long time. It combines my love of baking with my Amish-Mennonite heritage. The recipes are those that have been baked—indeed, are still being baked—by old-fashioned cooks in Amish and Mennonite communities across this great nation of ours. Many of these wonderful recipes have been handed down from generation to generation, often by word of mouth, leading to slight variations as they traveled from kitchen to kitchen. I have often watched my mother or grandmother put her own twist on an old family recipe, and I continue to do the same. If you have a traditional recipe that varies from mine, it doesn't mean that mine is right and yours is wrong (or vice versa), it just means that our recipes differ, although the essence of what we are baking remains the same.

My grandparents were part of the migration of Mennonites who came here from Europe and Russia to escape religious persecution. My parents were raised as Mennonites, learning the Low German (Plattdeutsch) that was spoken in their homes. Coming from similar backgrounds, they attended and met at Tabor College, a Mennonite school, in Hillsboro, Kansas, one of the oldest settlements of Low German Mennonites who migrated to America from Russia in the 1700s and the site of the first organized Mennonite Brethren Church in North America. After school they married and moved far away from their brethren to the islands of Hawaii, where they joined the First Foreign Church, originally founded by the missionaries you may have read about in James M. Michener's book *Hawaii*. Since all of this happened before I was born, I was not myself raised as a Mennonite. My dad was quite the storyteller, however, and I heard tales of my family and ancestors as I grew up. My mother, of course, continued to cook many of the Mennonite favorites that both she and my father had enjoyed growing up.

The Amish and Mennonite groups share a common heritage in European Anabaptism,* which originated in Switzerland. The Anabaptists

---

*Anabaptism is the belief that infants should not be baptized, but that young adults should make a conscious decision to join the church and not be baptized until that time.

formed what was then considered a "radical" wing of Protestantism. They rejected the state church, infant baptism, the swearing of oaths, and militarism. A Dutch priest named Menno Simons left the Catholic Church in 1536, and through his teachings and writings he became the leader of the Anabaptists. This led to their being named Mennonites. In 1693 a conservative Swiss Anabaptist Jacob Amman, fearing that the Mennonites were becoming too worldly, led his followers to split away from them, insisting on very strict conformity to ritualistic and social practices. They became known as the Amish.

Because of their beliefs, both groups were victims of religious persecution, causing them to seek freedom to practice their religion. This led to migrations across Europe and even into parts of Russia, where they were given a temporary reprieve from military service in return for working the land. They began migrating to America in the late 1600s. By the late 1800s, when their exemption from military service in Russia was threatened, the exodus from Europe and Russia accelerated.

The Mennonites and Amish often traveled together on the same ships. They live today as friendly and cooperating neighbors. As a group, the Amish are more strict than the Mennonites, but each individual church is ruled by the decisions of their elders. To the outside observer, a member of a strict Old Order Mennonite church may be indistinguishable from a member of the Amish order.

The Amish—and, to a lesser degree, the Mennonites—are plain and simple people in both dress and manner, although they add color to their lives with the cultivation of their flowers and in the design of their quilts. Colorful flowers are allowed not only in the garden but also in the home and are accepted as lovely gifts from God. I have not found a reasonable explanation for the bold color typically used in Amish quilting, but this lack of information cannot keep us from enjoying their beauty.

The kitchen is the heart of the Amish and Mennonite home, and it is the almost-daily baking that occurs there that is of the most importance. The hausfrau, reserved by nature, expresses much of her love for her family with wonderful baking. One does not need to be Amish or Mennonite, however, to appreciate that good food, especially good baking, brings families together.

My family and I had a grand time deciding which of the wonderful things we baked to include in this book. Every day the kitchen was filled with yeasty aromas and the sweetness of vanilla, cinnamon, and other spices. The result is not a scientifically gathered group of recipes. It is, instead, a personal collection of favorites. There is a bias toward the recipes of my own family's heritage, since many hark back to the dishes I enjoyed in my own home and in those of aunts, uncles, and cousins. But, just as in many of those early Kansas kitchens, there is also a sprinkling here of favorites from the Amish, the Pennsylvania Dutch, and Mennonites from other areas.

So, sit yourself down and eat yourself full. From my kitchen to yours—enjoy!

A Wooden Spoon
Baking Memoir

Old-Fashioned Cakes

There is nothing pretentious about any of these cakes. The Angel, Sunshine, Hot Milk Sponge, and Dutch Butter cakes are unadorned and can be served with sliced fruit in place of icing. The Chocolate Birthday Cake, of course, is frosted, as is the One-Egg Cake. Both merit repeated baking. Eins Zwei Drei Cake is typical of the flat cakes served at a Mennonite wedding. For every day, I like it with ice cream and chocolate syrup. The rest—Oatmeal, Applesauce, Shoofly, Rosy Rhubarb, Dutch Honey, and German Ginger cakes are all homey creations that will keep you coming back for more.

Angel Cake

Angel Cake, or Angel Food Cake, is thought to have originated with the Pennsylvania Dutch. It was created, no doubt, to use leftover egg whites after the yolks had been used in the making of noodles.

> 1¼ cups cake flour, sifted before measuring
> 1¾ cups granulated sugar
> 1⅔ cups egg whites (from 12 to 13 large eggs)
> 1 tablespoon warm water
> ¼ teaspoon salt
> 1½ teaspoons cream of tartar
> 1 teaspoon vanilla extract
> ½ teaspoon almond extract

1. Place the oven rack in the bottom third of the oven. Preheat to 360°F.

2. Sift the flour and ¾ cup of the sugar together 3 times. Set aside.

3. In the large bowl of an electric mixer, beat the egg whites with the warm water and salt at high speed until foamy. Sprinkle the

cream of tartar over the whites and beat until soft peaks form. Sprinkle the remaining cup of sugar over the whites, 1 tablespoon at a time, until all is used, beating all the while. The whites should be stiff but not dry. Remove the bowl from the mixer.

4. Sprinkle the vanilla and almond extracts over the egg white batter and fold in gently. Sprinkle the flour mixture over the whites, ¼ cup at a time, folding in gently after each addition. Spoon the batter into an ungreased 10-inch tube pan. Use a spatula to spread evenly. Bake in the oven for 35 to 40 minutes, or until the top springs back when touched lightly in the center.

5. Cool the cake in the pan for 1 hour, inverted on legs and neck. (If your pan has no legs, invert the neck over a bottle.) Remove the cake with a long thin knife and cool completely on a wire rack.

MAKES 12 SERVINGS.

Sunshine Cake

If you want to make Angel Cake (see page 3) but don't want to make noodles with the yolks, put them into this delicious cake. Slices of the two cakes are attractive served side by side on a platter.

2 cups cake flour, sifted before measuring
2 teaspoons baking powder
¼ teaspoon salt
⅔ cup egg yolks (from 11 to 12 large eggs)
2 cups granulated sugar
2 teaspoons vanilla extract
1 cup milk

1. Place the oven rack in the bottom third of the oven. Preheat to 350°F.

2. Sift the cake flour, baking powder, and salt together and set aside.

3. In the large bowl of an electric mixer, beat the egg yolks at medium-high speed until light and lemon colored. Gradually add the sugar, beating all the while.

4. Reduce mixer speed to low. Sprinkle the vanilla over the batter and mix in. Add the dry ingredients alternately with the milk, beginning and ending with the dry (4 parts dry, 3 parts milk). Use a spatula to scrape down the sides of the bowl as needed. Spoon the batter into an ungreased 10-inch tube pan. Spread evenly with a spatula. Bake in the oven for 50 to 60 minutes, or until the top springs back when lightly touched in the center.

5. Cool the cake in the pan for 1 hour, inverted on legs and neck. (If your pan has no legs, invert the neck over a bottle.) Remove the cake with a long thin knife and cool completely on a wire rack.

MAKES 12 SERVINGS.

Baking for a Mennonite Wedding

In the early years of American Mennonite communities, it was the custom to invite the entire congregation to a wedding. The invitation was extended from the pulpit on a Sunday morning. Food preparation was started days ahead of the ceremony. The cookies were baked first, followed by the zweiback and the kuchen or wedding cakes. It was impossible for the bride's parents to have enough butter, cream, and eggs on hand for all the baking. The sharing of these staples by friends and neighbors was as natural as helping with the work. The house was thoroughly cleaned. Silverware, dishes, tables, and chairs were borrowed and set up all over the house to accommodate the guests. One bedroom was left intact to display wedding gifts. Not having room to seat all the guests at once, the men were fed first. The children were fed separately (outside, if the weather was warm). The women, who did all the work, fed themselves last.

I know enough about my parents' wedding to almost feel I was there—certainly enough to wish I had been. They were married on November 25, 1926, in the bride's home in Buhler, Kansas. The wedding was officiated by P. E. Nickel, pastor of the Mennonite Brethren Church of Hillsboro, Kansas. On the marriage license my dad listed his age as twenty-one, my mother twenty, although, in truth, she was three months older than he. The late fall wedding was typical in the Mennonite farming community, coming after all crops were harvested and the fall farmwork was completed. I'm not sure that this was the reason my parents chose the date, however. My dad had been expelled from Tabor College for a prank involving his entering the women's dorm dressed as a girl, complete with a rag-mop wig. Innocent enough, as far as my father was concerned, but not to be tolerated at Tabor. Mother left the campus when he did, and the date simply may have been a convenient one to allow them to get on with their lives.

The wedding was an all-day affair—both lunch and supper were served. Friends and family came from near and far, and they needed to be fed. The wedding flowers were simple bouquets of chrysanthemums. The cake was homemade, without elaborate decorations. In contrast to some modern wedding cakes, it was more important that it taste "wonderful good," than that it be "too fancy." In my parents' day, such a cake would have been baked only in flat sheet pans and would have been more like Eins Zwei Drei Cake than a more modern tiered wedding cake.

Eins Zwei Drei Cake

Eins zwei drei means "one, two, three," referring to the measurements of the ingredients, making the recipe an easy one for a young Amish-Mennonite cook to memorize. It's a tender cake that's a wonderful foundation for ice creams and sauces.

> *1 cup (2 sticks) unsalted butter, softened*
> *1 cup granulated sugar*
> *3 large eggs*
> *1 teaspoon vanilla extract*
> *2 cups cake flour, sifted before measuring*
> *1 teaspoon baking powder*
> *¼ teaspoon salt*
> *¼ teaspoon ground nutmeg or mace*
> *Powdered sugar, optional*

1. Preheat the oven to 350°F. Grease a 10 × 15 × 1-inch jelly roll pan.

2. In a mixing bowl, beat the butter and sugar with a wooden spoon until light and fluffy. Add the eggs, one at a time, beating well after each. Mix in the vanilla. In another bowl, stir the flour with the baking powder, salt, and nutmeg; then stir into the butter mixture, ½ cup at a time.

3. Spread the dough evenly in the prepared pan. Bake in the preheated oven for 20 to 25 minutes, or until the cake begins to pull away from the sides of the pan. Cool in the pan on a wire rack. If desired, sift a little powdered sugar over the cake while it is still slightly warm. Serve squares of the cake with vanilla ice cream and chocolate or a fruit sauce.

MAKES 24 SERVINGS.

Chocolate Birthday Cake

My mother never had to "get out" a recipe to bake her chocolate cakes. She had learned how to make them by heart—as did all young Mennonite girls—as she worked side by side with her mother in their Kansas kitchen. This one, with a creamy chocolate frosting, is one of my favorites.

CAKE
¾ cup white vegetable shortening
1 cup granulated sugar
¾ cup light brown sugar, firmly packed
3 large eggs
2 teaspoons vanilla extract
2 cups bleached all-purpose flour
½ cup unsweetened cocoa powder
1 teaspoon salt
1½ teaspoons baking soda
1 cup milk
½ cup hot brewed coffee

FROSTING
1 pound (3¾ cups) powdered sugar
½ cup unsweetened cocoa powder
½ cup (1 stick) unsalted butter, softened
1 teaspoon vanilla extract
4 to 6 tablespoons hot brewed coffee

1. Prepare the cake: Preheat the oven to 350°F. Grease and flour two 9-inch round cake pans.

2. In a large mixing bowl, beat the shortening and granulated sugar with a wooden spoon until light and fluffy. Add the light brown sugar and beat again. Add the eggs, one at a time, beating well after each. Stir in the 2 teaspoons vanilla. In another bowl, sift or whisk the flour, ½ cup cocoa, salt, and baking soda together. Add to the batter alternately with the milk (3 parts dry ingredients, 2 parts milk). Stir in the ½ cup of hot coffee.

3. Spoon the batter into the prepared pans and bake in the oven for 30 minutes, or until the cake just begins to pull away from the sides of the pans. Let cool in the pans for 2 to 3 minutes and then turn out to cool on wire racks.

4. When the cake layers are cooled, prepare the frosting: In a large mixing bowl, sift or whisk together the powdered sugar and the ½ cup of cocoa. With a wooden spoon, beat in the butter and the 1 teaspoon vanilla. Add 4 to 6 tablespoons of hot coffee gradually to make a soft, fluffy frosting. Place the bottom layer of the cake on the serving plate and frost the top of that layer. Place the second layer on top of the first. Frost the sides of the cake and then the top.

MAKES 12 SERVINGS.

Hot Milk Sponge Cake

This is a quick little cake that's good with sweetened fresh fruit and cream—perfect for strawberry season. The recipe can be doubled to make a two-layer cake suitable for frosting.

> ¾ *cup bleached all-purpose flour*
> ¾ *teaspoon baking powder*
> ¼ *teaspoon salt*
> ⅓ *cup milk*
> 1 *tablespoon unsalted butter*
> 2 *large eggs*
> ¾ *cup granulated sugar*
> ½ *teaspoon vanilla extract*

1. Preheat the oven to 350°F. Grease a 9-inch round layer cake pan. Line the bottom of the pan with waxed paper. Grease the paper and then lightly flour the paper-lined pan.

2. Sift the flour, baking powder, and salt together and set aside. (I know you are used to *not* sifting flour these days, but this cake has a better texture if the dry ingredients are sifted.)

3. In a small saucepan heat the milk and the butter together until the milk is hot and the butter is melted. Remove from heat.

4. In the large bowl of a mixer, beat the eggs until thick. Gradually add the sugar, beating all the while. At low speed, blend in the vanilla, then the dry ingredients, then the hot milk mixture. Pour the batter into the prepared baking pan and bake in the oven for 25 to 30 minutes, or until the cake springs back when lightly touched in the center. Cool in the pan, elevated on a wire rack, for 5 minutes. Turn out on the rack and peel the paper from the bottom of the cake. Reinvert on another rack to cool completely.

MAKES 6 SERVINGS.

One-Egg Cake

This simple little cake, baked "when the hens weren't laying and eggs were scarce," makes a fine family dessert. Actually, I wouldn't be ashamed to serve it to company.

CAKE
½ cup white vegetable shortening
1 cup granulated sugar
1 large egg
1 teaspoon vanilla extract
1¾ cups bleached all-purpose flour
2½ teaspoons baking powder
¼ teaspoon salt
¾ cup milk

FROSTING
3 cups powdered sugar
4 tablespoons unsalted butter, softened
3 to 5 tablespoons brewed coffee, cooled to room temperature

1. Preheat the oven to 350°F. Grease and flour two 8-inch round cake pans.

2. Prepare the cake: In a mixing bowl, beat the shortening and granulated sugar with a wooden spoon until light and fluffy. Add the egg and vanilla and beat again. Sift or whisk together the flour, baking powder, and salt. Add the dry ingredients to the batter alternately with the milk (3 parts dry ingredients, 2 parts milk), mixing well after each addition. Spoon the batter into the prepared pans, spreading it evenly. Bake in the oven for 20 to 25 minutes, or until the cake springs back when lightly touched in the center. Invert the cake layers on wire racks. Remove the pans. Invert layers again to cool completely on the racks.

3. Prepare the frosting: In a small bowl, beat the powdered sugar and butter together until smooth. Gradually add the coffee to make a spreadable frosting. Spread the frosting on top of one layer. Stack the other layer on top of the first and spread the frosting on the sides. Spread the remaining frosting on the top of the cake.

MAKES 12 SERVINGS.

Dutch Butter Cake

This is not unlike a pound cake, and it is delicious.

1 cup (2 sticks) unsalted butter, softened
1¼ cups granulated sugar
5 large eggs
1 tablespoon vanilla extract
2 cups bleached all-purpose flour
¼ teaspoon salt
¼ teaspoon baking powder
¼ teaspoon ground nutmeg

1. Have all ingredients at room temperature before you begin. If your eggs are cold, they can be brought to room temperature by immersing them in warm water for about 10 minutes. Drain them on paper toweling to dry. Preheat the oven to 325°F. Grease and flour a 9 × 5-inch loaf pan.

2. In a mixing bowl beat the butter with a wooden spoon until soft and creamy. Add the sugar, ¼ cup at a time, beating well after each addition. Add the eggs, one at a time, beating well after each. Stir in the vanilla. Sift or whisk the flour, salt, baking powder, and nutmeg together. Add the flour mixture to the batter, ¼ cup at a time, folding and stirring gently after each addition. (The batter may look curdled when you begin, but it should look creamy by the time the last of the dry ingredients are added.)

3. Spoon the batter into the prepared pan. Spread evenly with a spatula. Bake in the oven for 1 to 1¼ hours, or until a wooden pick inserted in the center comes out clean. Cool in the pan 5 minutes. Turn out to cool completely on a wire rack.

MAKES 12 SERVINGS.

Why the Amish Use Buggies

It was pointed out in a film shown at the Menno-Hof Visitor's Center in Shipshewana that a car costs an average of $15,000, while a buggy costs but $3,000. The average car owner will buy ten vehicles in his lifetime, the Amishman but three. The primary reason the Amish prefer buggies, however, is that a car can go too far too easily, taking their brethren away from their community in more ways than one. An old Amish farmer was asked why he used a buggy for travel when it could not take him all the way to the big city. He answered, "That's why."

Oatmeal Cake

Oatmeal Cake combines the texture of cake with the flavor of an oatmeal cookie. Baked in a flat pan with the icing broiled right on top of the cake, it is delightfully easy and quick to make.

CAKE
1 cup uncooked old-fashioned or quick oatmeal (not instant)
1¼ cups boiling water
½ cup white vegetable shortening
¾ cup granulated sugar
¾ cup light brown sugar, firmly packed
2 large eggs
1 teaspoon vanilla extract
1½ cups bleached all-purpose flour
½ teaspoon salt
1 teaspoon baking soda
1 teaspoon ground cinnamon
¼ teaspoon ground nutmeg

ICING
6 tablespoons unsalted butter
¼ cup evaporated milk
1 teaspoon vanilla extract
1 cup light brown sugar, firmly packed
1 cup sweetened flaked coconut
1 cup chopped pecans (optional)

1. Preheat the oven to 350°F. Grease a 9 × 13-inch baking pan.

2. Prepare the cake: In a small bowl stir the oatmeal and boiling water together. Let stand until cool while proceeding with the recipe.

3. In a mixing bowl beat the shortening and the granulated sugar with a wooden spoon until light and fluffy. Add the ¾ cup light brown sugar and beat again. Add the eggs and the 1 teaspoon vanilla and beat again. Stir in the oatmeal mixture. Sift or whisk together in a mixing bowl the flour, salt, baking soda, cinnamon, and nutmeg, then stir this

into the batter. Spread evenly in the prepared pan and bake for 25 to 30 minutes, or until the top springs back when lightly touched in the center.

4. Meanwhile, prepare the icing (you want the icing ready to go on the cake just when it comes out of the oven): In a medium saucepan combine the butter, evaporated milk, 1 teaspoon vanilla, and 1 cup light brown sugar. Stir over medium heat until the butter melts and the mixture is smooth. Remove from heat. Stir in the coconut and pecans. Immediately spread the icing on the hot cake. Place the cake 3 inches below the broiler and broil until the icing is bubbly and golden, 2 to 5 minutes. Cool on a wire rack.

MAKES 12 SERVINGS.

Applesauce Cake

The first time I made Applesauce Cake, I was well into the recipe before I realized my pantry contained no applesauce. I called a relative who lived close by, and she offered some of her "home-canned." My cake was a great success. Luckily, the recipe works as well with sauce packed in jars found at the supermarket.

> *½ cup white vegetable shortening*
> *1 cup granulated sugar*
> *1 large egg*
> *1¾ cups bleached all-purpose flour*
> *½ teaspoon salt*
> *½ teaspoon baking soda*
> *1 teaspoon baking powder*
> *1 teaspoon ground cinnamon*
> *¼ teaspoon ground nutmeg*
> *1 to 1¼ cups applesauce (use the greater amount only if your*
> *   applesauce is very chunky or dry)*

1. Preheat the oven to 350°F. Grease and flour a 9 × 5-inch loaf pan.

2. In a mixing bowl beat the shortening and the granulated sugar with a wooden spoon until light and fluffy. Add the egg and beat again.

14

3. Sift or whisk together in a small mixing bowl the flour, salt, baking soda, baking powder, cinnamon, and nutmeg. Add to the batter alternately with the applesauce (3 parts dry ingredients, 2 parts applesauce). Spoon into the prepared pan and smooth the top with the back of a wooden spoon. Bake in the oven for about 1 hour, or until a wooden pick inserted in the center comes out clean.

4. Let cool in the pan for 3 minutes. Turn out to cool completely on a wire rack.

MAKES 12 SERVINGS.

Shoofly Cake

This cake is one of my family's absolute favorites. They love the moistness of the cake with its spicy molasses flavor. It is made similarly to traditional Pennsylvania Dutch Shoofly Pie (page 51). The liquid is a mixture of water and molasses. The crumbs are spiced to give a hint of gingerbread. The whole thing goes together rather quickly.

4 cups bleached all-purpose flour
2 cups light brown sugar, firmly packed
½ teaspoon salt
1 teaspoon ground cinnamon
¼ teaspoon ground nutmeg
¼ teaspoon ground ginger
¼ teaspoon ground cloves
1 cup (2 sticks) unsalted butter, softened
2 cups boiling water
1 cup unsulphured molasses
2 teaspoons baking soda

1. Preheat the oven to 350°F. Butter a 9 × 12 × 2-inch glass baking dish.

2. In a small bowl stir together the flour, light brown sugar, salt, cinnamon, nutmeg, ginger, and cloves. Cut in the butter until the mixture is reduced to fine crumbs. Lightly spoon out 1½ cups of the crumbs for topping.

15

3. In a separate bowl, stir the boiling water and molasses together. Sprinkle the baking soda over the molasses mixture. Add the crumbs remaining in the small bowl and stir just to mix. The batter will be thin with only a few lumps remaining. Pour into the prepared baking dish. Sprinkle the reserved crumbs over the top.

4. Bake in the preheated oven for 35 to 40 minutes, or until a wooden pick inserted in the center comes out clean. Cool in the pan on a wire rack. Serve slightly warm or at room temperature.

MAKES 12 TO 16 SERVINGS.

Rosy Rhubarb Cake

Some people don't like rhubarb because it's so tart, but sugar fixes that. This sweet cake with its cinnamony topping proves a great foil for the tartness of the rhubarb.

TOPPING
½ cup bleached all-purpose flour
⅓ cup granulated sugar
½ teaspoon ground cinnamon
4 tablespoons unsalted butter

CAKE
½ cup white vegetable shortening
1 cup granulated sugar
1 large egg, beaten
1 teaspoon vanilla extract
2 cups bleached all-purpose flour
2 teaspoons baking powder
½ teaspoon salt
½ teaspoon ground cinnamon
¾ cup plus 2 tablespoons milk
3 cups finely sliced rhubarb

1. Preheat the oven to 350°F. Grease a 9 × 13-inch pan.

2. Prepare the topping: Mix together the ½ cup flour, ⅓ cup sugar, and ½ teaspoon cinnamon. Cut in the 4 tablespoons butter to make fine crumbs. Set aside.

3. Prepare the cake: In a mixing bowl, beat the shortening with a wooden spoon until soft and fluffy. Gradually add the 1 cup sugar, beating well. Add the egg and the vanilla and stir to blend.

4. Sift or whisk together in a bowl the 2 cups flour, baking powder, salt, and ½ teaspoon cinnamon. Add to the shortening mixture alternately with the milk (3 parts dry ingredients, 2 parts milk), blending well after each addition. Fold in the sliced rhubarb.

5. Spread in the greased pan. Sprinkle the topping evenly over the batter. Bake in the preheated oven for 45 minutes, or until the top is lightly browned and a wooden pick inserted in the center comes out clean. Cool in the pan on a wire rack. Serve slightly warm or at room temperature.

MAKES 12 TO 16 SERVINGS.

Dutch Honey Cake

The succulence of apricots combines with the sweet flavor of honey to make this a most pleasing cake. Some bakers use twice the honey that I do, but I find cakes made this way are so rich, they are more likely to collapse than to hold their shape.

> *1 package (6 ounces) dried apricots*
> *1½ cups boiling water*
> *½ cup white vegetable shortening*
> *½ cup granulated sugar*
> *½ cup honey*
> *3 large eggs*
> *2 cups bleached all-purpose flour*
> *½ teaspoon salt*
> *2½ teaspoons baking powder*
> *1 teaspoon ground cinnamon*
> *½ cup milk*

1. Preheat the oven to 350°F. Grease and flour a 9 × 5-inch loaf pan.

2. With a kitchen scissors, snip the apricots into pieces the size of raisins. Cover with the boiling water and let stand for 10 minutes. Drain well.

3. In a mixing bowl beat the shortening and sugar with a wooden spoon until light and fluffy. Add the honey and beat again. Add the eggs, one at a time, beating well after each. Sift or whisk together in another bowl the flour, salt, baking powder, and cinnamon and add to the batter alternately with the milk (3 parts dry ingredients, 2 parts milk). Fold in the drained apricots.

4. Spoon the batter into the pan, spreading evenly with a spatula. Bake in the oven for 50 to 60 minutes, or until a wooden pick inserted in the center comes out clean. Cool in the pan 5 minutes. Turn out to cool completely on a wire rack. Serve slices of the cake with sherbet or ice cream.

MAKES 12 SERVINGS.

German Ginger Cake
with Raisin Sauce

When you grow up with desserts like this, you develop a taste for molasses, brown sugar, and raisins. Delicious!

CAKE

½ cup white vegetable shortening
½ cup granulated sugar
½ cup unsulphured molasses
1 large egg
1¾ cups bleached all-purpose flour
¼ teaspoon salt
1 teaspoon baking soda
¾ teaspoon ground ginger
¾ teaspoon ground cinnamon
⅔ cup boiling water

SAUCE

1 cup warm water
½ cup raisins
¾ cup light brown sugar, firmly packed
1 tablespoon cornstarch
¼ teaspoon ground cinnamon
¼ cup cider vinegar
1 tablespoon unsalted butter, softened

1. Preheat the oven to 350°F. Grease an 8 × 8 × 2-inch baking pan.

2. Prepare the cake: In a mixing bowl beat the shortening and the granulated sugar with a wooden spoon until well blended. Add the molasses and beat again. Add the egg and beat until blended.

3. Sift or whisk together in another bowl the flour, salt, baking soda, ginger, and the ¾ teaspoon cinnamon. Add half the dry ingredients to the batter and stir until mixed. Add half the boiling water; stir

19

until mixed. Repeat, using the remaining dry ingredients and boiling water. Transfer to the baking pan and bake in the oven for 30 to 35 minutes, or until the top springs back when lightly touched in the center.

4. Prepare the sauce: In a small saucepan combine the warm water and the raisins. Bring to a simmer and cook for 5 minutes. Remove from heat.

5. In a medium saucepan away from heat stir together the light brown sugar, cornstarch, and the ¼ teaspoon cinnamon. Stir in the vinegar, then the hot raisin mixture. Cook over medium heat, stirring constantly, until thickened, 2 to 3 minutes. Remove from heat. Add the butter and stir to melt and mix. Serve squares of warm cake with the sauce poured over the top.

MAKES 9 SERVINGS.

Lunch Box
Cupcakes

Cupcakes have always been one of my favorite desserts, back when my mother packed them in my school lunch box, too many years ago to remember, and now when I brown-bag it to work. They are the perfect-sized cake, already wrapped and topped with a swirl of frosting—what more could you ask for?

Most layer cake recipes can be adapted to make cupcakes. Batter for a two-layer cake will make about 24 cupcakes. Just fill paper-lined muffin pan cups ⅔ to ¾ full and bake at 350 to 375°F for 15 to 20 minutes.

Yellow Cupcakes

These are rich little butter cakes with a pure vanilla frosting. You can put one in my lunch box any day.

CUPCAKES
½ cup unsalted butter, softened
1¼ cups granulated sugar
2 large eggs
1 teaspoon vanilla extract
2¼ cups cake flour, sifted before measuring
1 tablespoon baking powder
½ teaspoon salt
⅔ cup milk

FROSTING
2¾ cups powdered sugar
3 tablespoons unsalted butter, softened
1 teaspoon vanilla extract
2 to 4 tablespoons milk

1. Preheat the oven to 350°F. Line 21 4-ounce muffin cups with paper liners.

2. Prepare the cupcakes: In a mixing bowl, beat the ½ cup butter and the granulated sugar with a wooden spoon until light and fluffy. Add the eggs, one at a time, beating well after each. Add the 1 teaspoon vanilla and beat again.

3. Sift or whisk together in a bowl the flour, baking powder, and salt. Add the flour mixture to the batter alternately with the ⅔ cup milk (3 parts dry ingredients, 2 parts milk). Spoon the batter into the lined muffin cups, filling ⅔ full. Bake in the oven for 20 to 25 minutes, or until a cupcake springs back when lightly touched in the center. Remove to cool on wire racks.

4. Prepare the frosting: Beat the powdered sugar, 3 tablespoons butter, and 1 teaspoon vanilla together until well blended. Gradually add the 2 to 4 tablespoons milk to make a spreadable mixture. Spread on the cooled cupcakes.

MAKES 21 CUPCAKES.

Cocoa Cupcakes

These are so easy to throw together—there's no excuse for not making them for your family.

CUPCAKES
1½ cups bleached all-purpose flour
1 cup granulated sugar
¼ cup unsweetened cocoa powder
½ teaspoon salt
1 teaspoon baking soda
1 teaspoon vanilla extract
1 teaspoon cider vinegar
⅓ cup canola oil
1 cup milk

FROSTING
2 cups powdered sugar
¼ cup unsweetened cocoa powder
4 tablespoons unsalted butter, softened
1 teaspoon vanilla extract
2 to 3 tablespoons milk

1. Preheat the oven to 350°F. Line 16 muffin cups with paper liners.

2. Prepare the cupcakes: In a mixing bowl with a pouring spout, sift or whisk together the flour, granulated sugar, ¼ cup cocoa, salt, and baking soda. Make a well in the dry ingredients. In that well place the 1 teaspoon vanilla, vinegar, oil, and 1 cup milk. Beat with a whisk or wooden spoon until smooth. A few small lumps are OK, but press out any large lumps that may remain.

3. Pour the batter into the paper-lined muffin cups. Bake in the preheated oven for about 20 minutes, or until the top of one cupcake springs back when lightly touched in the center. Remove from the pans and cool on wire racks. Frost when cool.

4. Prepare the frosting: In small mixing bowl, stir together the powdered sugar and ¼ cup cocoa. With a wooden spoon, beat in the butter and 1 teaspoon vanilla. Slowly stir in the 2 to 3 tablespoons milk to make a spreadable mixture. Spread on the tops of the cooled cupcakes.
MAKES 16 CUPCAKES.

Banana Cupcakes

I think these are good with or without frosting, but my grandchildren say, "Frosting, please."

CUPCAKES
½ cup white vegetable shortening
1 cup granulated sugar
½ cup light brown sugar, firmly packed
2 large eggs, slightly beaten
1 teaspoon vanilla extract
1 cup mashed banana
2 cups bleached all-purpose flour
½ teaspoon salt
1 teaspoon baking powder
½ teaspoon baking soda
1 teaspoon ground cinnamon
½ cup buttermilk

FROSTING
3 cups powdered sugar
4 tablespoons unsalted butter
1 teaspoon vanilla extract
2 to 4 tablespoons milk

1. Preheat the oven to 350°F. Line 24 muffin cups with paper liners.

2. Prepare the cupcakes: Beat the shortening with the granulated sugar until light and fluffy. Add the light brown sugar and beat again. Add the eggs, one at a time, beating well after each. Stir in the 1 teaspoon vanilla, then the banana.

3. Sift or whisk together in a bowl the flour, salt, baking powder, baking soda, and cinnamon. Add ½ of the flour mixture to the batter and stir to blend. Stir in the buttermilk. Stir in the remaining flour mixture. Spoon the batter into the lined muffin cups, filling ⅔ full. Bake in the oven for 20 to 25 minutes, or until the top of one cupcake springs

back when touched in the center. Remove from the pans and cool on wire racks.

4. Prepare the frosting: In a large bowl, beat the powdered sugar, the butter, and the 1 teaspoon vanilla with a wooden spoon until blended. Slowly add the 2 to 4 tablespoons milk to make a spreadable mixture. Spread on the tops of the cooled cupcakes.

MAKES 24 CUPCAKES.

Peanut Butter Cupcakes

These cupcakes combine the flavor of a peanut butter cookie with the texture of a butter cake. It's hard to stop with one.

CUPCAKES
½ cup white vegetable shortening
½ cup creamy peanut butter
⅔ cup granulated sugar
⅔ cup light brown sugar, firmly packed
2 large eggs
1 teaspoon vanilla extract
1½ cups bleached all-purpose flour
¼ teaspoon salt
2 teaspoons baking powder
⅔ cup milk

FROSTING
2½ cups powdered sugar
¼ cup unsweetened cocoa powder
4 tablespoons unsalted butter, softened
½ teaspoon vanilla extract
3 to 4 tablespoons milk

1. Preheat the oven to 350°F. Line 24 muffin cups with paper liners.

27

2. Prepare the cupcakes: In a large bowl, beat the shortening and the peanut butter with a wooden spoon until smooth. Add the granulated sugar and beat again. Add the light brown sugar and beat again. Add the eggs, one at a time, beating well after each. Blend in the 1 teaspoon vanilla. Sift or whisk together in a bowl the flour, salt, and baking powder, then add these ingredients alternately with the ⅔ cup milk (3 parts dry ingredients, 2 parts milk), blending well after each addition.

3. Spoon the batter into the paper-lined cups, filling each ⅔ full. Bake in the oven for 15 to 20 minutes, or until the top of a cupcake springs back when lightly touched in the center. Remove from the pans and cool on wire racks.

4. Prepare the frosting: In a small bowl stir together the powdered sugar and the cocoa. Add the butter and the ½ teaspoon vanilla and mix. Gradually add the 3 to 4 tablespoons milk to make a spreadable mixture. Spread on the tops of the cooled cupcakes.

MAKES 24 CUPCAKES.

Gingerbread Cupcakes

These cupcakes are put together the way I make all of my gingerbreads, with hot water stirred in at the end, making them nice and light. The spicy gingerbread goes well with the lemony frosting.

CUPCAKES
½ *cup white vegetable shortening*
¾ *cup granulated sugar*
2 *large eggs*
¾ *cup unsulphured molasses*
2½ *cups bleached all-purpose flour*
1 *teaspoon baking powder*
1 *teaspoon baking soda*
½ *teaspoon salt*
1 *tablespoon ground ginger*

1 teaspoon ground cinnamon
1 cup boiling water

FROSTING
3 cups powdered sugar
4 tablespoons butter, softened
1 tablespoon fresh lemon juice
2 to 3 tablespoons fresh orange juice

1. Preheat the oven to 350°F. Line 24 4-ounce muffin cups with paper liners.

2. Prepare the cupcakes: In a mixing bowl, beat the shortening and granulated sugar with a wooden spoon until light and fluffy. Add the eggs, one at a time, beating well after each. Stir in the molasses. Sift or whisk together in a bowl the flour, baking powder, baking soda, salt, ginger, and cinnamon. Add ½ of the dry ingredients to the batter and stir to mix. Add half the water and stir and fold to mix. Repeat with the remaining dry ingredients and water.

3. Spoon into the paper-lined cups, filling ⅔ full. Bake for 20 to 25 minutes, or until a cupcake springs back when lightly touched in the center. Transfer to wire racks to cool.

4. Prepare the frosting: In a medium-sized bowl beat the powdered sugar, butter, and lemon juice with a wooden spoon until smooth. Gradually add the orange juice to make a spreadable mixture. Spread on the cooled cupcakes.

MAKES 24 CUPCAKES.

Perfect Pies

I grew up eating leftover pie for breakfast, a habit I continue to enjoy. With a fruit pie, you can almost convince yourself it's good for you, and with the others, it's certainly no worse than a doughnut. All my favorites are here: fruit pies, such as Lattice-Topped Rhubarb, Rhubarb Cream, Winter Cherry, Dutch Apple, Sour Cream Apple, Raisin, and Fresh Strawberry; the old-fashioned favorites of Velvet, Poppy Seed, and Lemon Sponge; and unique pies, such as Apple Butter, Union, Vinegar, Gravel, Funny-Cake, Pennsylvania Dutch Shoofly, Amish Vanilla, Collage, and my all-time favorite Half-Moon.

Lattice-Topped Rhubarb Pie

Many women, as they mature, find themselves turning into their mothers. I think I'm becoming more like my grandma Nachtigal, who always appreciated the simple things in life. Maybe that's why I like this pie. The only fancy part of it is the lattice crust, and you can substitute a plain one if you prefer.

> *Pastry for a Double-Crust Pie (page 129)*
> *1¼ cups granulated sugar*
> *3 tablespoons quick-cooking tapioca*
> *4 cups thinly sliced fresh rhubarb*

1. Preheat oven to 425°F.

2. Roll out the pastry for the bottom crust. Line 9-inch pie pan with the pastry.

3. In a mixing bowl, stir together the sugar and tapioca. Add the rhubarb and toss to coat all pieces of the rhubarb with the sugar mixture. Transfer to the pastry-lined pie pan, scraping the bowl to get all the sugar mixture into the pie.

4. Roll out the top crust. Cut into ¾-inch strips. Weave strips on top of the pie to form a lattice crust. Fold the top edge over the bottom to seal and press the edges between your fingers to crimp. Bake in preheated oven for 35 to 40 minutes, or until the crust is browned and the filling bubbles. The edge of the crust will brown deeply. If you wish to avoid this, drape a thin strip of foil over edge, halfway through the baking time. Cool on a wire rack.

MAKES 6 TO 8 SERVINGS.

Rhubarb Cream Pie

There is no cream in this pie. It's the sugared eggs that make the filling so creamy. The pie is delicious.

TOPPING
½ cup bleached all-purpose flour
⅓ cup granulated sugar
6 tablespoons unsalted butter

PIE
Pastry for a Single-Crust Pie (page 129)
1½ cups granulated sugar
¼ cup bleached all-purpose flour
¼ teaspoon ground nutmeg
3 large eggs, slightly beaten
4 cups thinly sliced fresh rhubarb

1. Preheat the oven to 400°F.

2. Prepare the topping: In a bowl, mix the ½ cup flour with the ⅓ cup sugar. Cut in the butter to make fine crumbs. Set aside.

3. Prepare the pie: Roll out the pastry. Line a 9-inch pie pan with the pastry to form a pie shell. In another bowl mix the 1½ cups sugar with the ¼ cup flour and the nutmeg. Stir in the eggs and mix until smooth. Fold in the rhubarb. Spoon into the pie shell. Sprinkle the topping over the filling.

4. Bake in the preheated oven for about 40 minutes, or until the filling bubbles and the topping browns. Cool on a wire rack. Be sure to refrigerate leftovers.

MAKES 6 TO 8 SERVINGS.

Fresh Strawberry Pie

While touring the countryside near Arthur, Illinois, my husband and I stopped to check out an Amish market located between a farmhouse and the road. Next to the dates, prunes, and schnitz (dried apples), I spotted fruit-flavored gelatin in oversized bulk packages. The Amish do use quite a bit of fruit-flavored gelatin in their cooking, and, of course, buying it in bulk saves them money.

My Fresh Strawberry Pie, which uses a standard-sized box of strawberry gelatin, has a nice, light texture that preserves the just-picked flavor of the berries. You can use the same recipe for fresh peaches with orange-flavored gelatin (recipe follows).

Pastry for a Single-Crust Pie (page 129)
1 cup granulated sugar
2 tablespoons cornstarch
1½ cups cool water
1 package (3 ounces) strawberry-flavored gelatin
1 quart fresh strawberries, sliced (you should have about 2½
* cups sliced berries)*

1. Roll out the pastry. Line a 9-inch pie pan with the pastry to form a pie shell. Prick the dough generously with a fork all over the bottom and sides. Gently line the shell with regular-weight aluminum foil to keep the shell from losing shape. Bake in a 425°F oven for 6 minutes. Remove the foil. Bake for 7 to 9 minutes longer, or until lightly browned. Set aside to cool while making filling.

2. In a medium saucepan stir together the sugar and cornstarch. Stir in the water. Bring to a simmer, stirring constantly. Continue to cook,

stirring, until thickened, 1 to 2 minutes. Remove from heat. Stir in the gelatin.

3. Place the strawberries in the pie shell in an even layer. Pour the gelatin mixture over the berries, making sure to coat them all. Chill the pie to firm. Serve as is or with a dollop of whipped cream. Be sure to refrigerate leftovers.

MAKES 6 TO 8 SERVINGS.

Fresh Peach Pie

Follow the recipe for Fresh Strawberry Pie, substituting 2½ cups sliced fresh peaches (1 to 1½ pounds) for the strawberries and orange-flavored gelatin for the strawberry-flavored.

Raisin Pie

This old-fashioned raisin pie is freshened with a splash of lemon juice. You can use either dark or golden raisins in the filling. I sometimes use one cup of each.

> *2 cups raisins*
> *1¾ cups cool water*
> *⅔ cup granulated sugar*
> *3 tablespoons cornstarch*
> *Pinch salt*
> *¼ cup fresh lemon juice*
> *1 tablespoon unsalted butter, softened*
> *Pastry for a Double-Crust Pie (page 129)*

1. Preheat the oven to 400°F.

2. Put the raisins and water in a medium-size saucepan, cover, and cook until water comes to a boil, then simmer for 5 minutes. Remove from heat.

3. Stir together the sugar, cornstarch, and the salt in a large saucepan. Stir in the lemon juice, then the raisin and water mixture. Bring to

a simmer, stirring constantly. Continue to cook, stirring, until thickened, about 2 minutes. Remove from heat. Gently stir in the butter until melted. Let the raisin mixture cool until you can comfortably touch the bottom of the pan.

4. Roll out the pastry for the bottom crust and line a 9-inch pie pan. Spoon the raisin filling into the crust. Roll out and fit the top crust. Fold the top edge over the bottom to seal and press the edges between your fingers to crimp. Cut slashes in the top crust for the escape of steam. Bake in the preheated oven for 30 to 35 minutes, or until the filling is bubbling and the crust is browned. Let the pie cool before serving to allow the filling to firm. Chill for an even firmer texture.

MAKES 6 TO 8 SERVINGS.

Dutch Apple Pie

When the weather warms in early summer, I take off for Shipshewana, a major Amish-Mennonite community in northern Indiana. Traveling the back roads, I pass rather plain white clapboard houses, unmarred by electrical poles or wires. Up near the road are large vegetable gardens bordered with brightly colored flowers. Side yards boast clotheslines hung with dark trousers, blue shirts, and dusty-colored dresses, announcing my arrival in Amish country.

The day always begins with a visit to Yoder's Department Store. Yoder's is a great big barn of a place. The center of the store is a wide open aisle, partitioned from the sales floor by a hip-high railing. On one side of this railing is the dry goods department, on the other, the hardware. I always look over the hardware first, marveling at the ingenuity of hand-powered kitchen gadgets for the Amish housewife who does without electricity. Then I cross over to the dry goods department. After walking through the displays of wide-brimmed hats, dark trousers, and sensible shoes, I find the piece goods section where I can browse to my heart's content. Often as not, I come away with several yards of solid and printed cottons for a quilt.

By the time I've finished at Yoder's, I've worked up an appetite for lunch. There are several good restaurants in Shipshewana, and I don't care which I go to as long as they have Dutch Apple Pie on the menu. It is *the* classic crumb-topped pie—filled with tart apples and topped with sugary crumbs—heaven.

PIE

Pastry for a Single-Crust Pie (page 129)
¾ cup granulated sugar
3 tablespoons bleached all-purpose flour
1 teaspoon ground cinnamon
6 cups peeled, cored, quartered, and sliced tart apples
1 tablespoon fresh lemon juice

CRUMB TOPPING

6 tablespoons light brown sugar, firmly packed
6 tablespoons bleached all-purpose flour
3 tablespoons unsalted butter, softened

1. Preheat the oven to 450°F.

2. Prepare the pie: Roll out pastry. Line a pie pan with the pastry. Trim and flute the edges.

3. In a bowl mix together the granulated sugar, 3 tablespoons flour, and the cinnamon. Add the apples and toss to mix. Place in the pie shell. Sprinkle with the lemon juice.

4. Prepare the topping: In a bowl mix the brown sugar and the 6 tablespoons flour together. Cut in the butter to make crumbs. Sprinkle the crumbs evenly over the top of the apples. Bake in the preheated oven for 10 minutes. Reduce the heat to 350°F and bake for 30 minutes longer. Cool on a wire rack.

MAKES 6 TO 8 SERVINGS.

Sour Cream Apple Pie

This pie is a delicate balance of flavors and textures. The apple slices, encased in a smooth vanilla-flavored sour cream custard filling, retain their individual shape, texture, and flavor while cooking. The slightly tart tones of the apples and the sour cream are moderated by the sugar in both the filling and the cinnamony topping. The result is that while you are finishing your first piece, you are already thinking about your second.

PIE

¾ cup granulated sugar

3 tablespoons bleached all-purpose flour

Pinch salt

3 cups peeled, cored, and thinly sliced tart apples

1 large egg

1 cup sour cream

1 teaspoon vanilla extract

Pastry for a Single-Crust Pie (page 129)

TOPPING

1 tablespoon granulated sugar

½ teaspoon ground cinnamon

1. Preheat the oven to 375°F.

2. Prepare the pie: In a mixing bowl stir the ¾ cup sugar together with the flour and the salt. Add the apples and toss to coat the apples with the sugar mixture.

3. In a small bowl beat the egg until smooth. Stir in the sour cream and vanilla. Stir this mixture into the apple mixture. Roll out pastry. Line a 9-inch pie pan with the pastry to form a pie shell. Spoon the apple mixture into the pie shell.

4. Prepare the topping: Stir together the 1 tablespoon sugar and the cinnamon, and then sprinkle this over the top of the pie. Bake in the oven for 35 to 40 minutes, or until the filling is set and the top is browned. Cool on a wire rack. Serve at room temperature or chilled. Be sure to refrigerate leftovers.

MAKES 6 TO 8 SERVINGS.

Canning

Most Amish and Mennonites live close to the land, and a goal of self-sufficiency leads to constant canning during harvest. Canned fruits and preserves not only stand alone but often find their way into the cakes, breads, and pies that are baked the following winter. The typical cellar of an Amish or Mennonite farmer's family would contain the following:

110 quarts applesauce
48 quarts sliced peaches
15 quarts blueberries
12 quarts strawberries
12 quarts peas
48 quarts string beans
40 quarts sweet corn
13 quarts bread-and-butter pickles
31 quarts garlic dill pickles
14 quarts sweet pickles
10 quarts mustard pickles
8 quarts pickled beets
15 pints pickle relish
10 pints corn relish
61 quarts tomato juice
25 quarts whole tomatoes
25 pints catsup
6 pints tomato butter
22 pints apple butter
6 pints blueberry jam
8 pints pear honey (actually preserves)
12 pints grape jelly
10 quarts grape juice

Winter Cherry Pie

When I was growing up, we didn't live in the right climate for growing a cherry tree, so my mother made her cherry pies with store-bought canned fruit. If she had had a tree, her winter cherry pies would have been made with fruit she had canned herself. My tasters told me that this simple recipe produced the best cherry pie they have ever eaten.

2 cans (16 ounces each) red tart pitted cherries
1¼ cups granulated sugar
2½ tablespoons quick-cooking tapioca
Pinch of salt
¼ teaspoon almond extract
1 tablespoon fresh lemon juice
Pastry for Double-Crust Pie (page 129)
1 tablespoon unsalted butter

1. Preheat the oven to 400°F.

2. Drain the cherries well, reserving ¼ cup of the juice.

3. In a mixing bowl stir together the sugar, tapioca, and salt. Add the almond extract, lemon juice, and reserved cherry juice and stir again. Stir in the cherries. Let stand while preparing the pie pastry.

4. Roll out the pastry. Line a 9-inch pie plate with the bottom crust. Spoon in the filling. Dot with slivers of the butter. Cover with the top crust. Fold the top edge over the bottom to seal and press the edges between your fingers to crimp. With a small sharp knife, cut several leaf shapes and small circles (to resemble cherries) out of the top crust. Bake for 45 to 50 minutes, or until the filling is bubbling and the crust is browned. Cool on a wire rack.

MAKES 6 TO 8 SERVINGS.

Mock Mince Pie

This pie combines two fruits of early autumn—freshly picked tart apples and green tomatoes that fruit too late to ripen. It's a great substitute for mince pie made with meat.

> *Pastry for Double-Crust Pie (page 129)*
> *1 cup light brown sugar, firmly packed*
> *2 tablespoons bleached all-purpose flour*
> *1 teaspoon ground cinnamon*
> *¼ teaspoon ground cloves*
> *2 cups chopped unpeeled green tomatoes, well drained*
> *2 cups peeled, cored, and chopped tart apples*
> *1 cup raisins*
> *1 tablespoon cider vinegar*
> *1 tablespoon unsalted butter*

1. Preheat the oven to 450°F.

2. Roll out the bottom crust and fit into a 9-inch pie pan.

3. In a mixing bowl, stir together the light brown sugar, flour, cinnamon, and cloves. Add the tomatoes, apples, and raisins and toss to coat the fruit with the dry ingredients. Transfer to the pie pan. Sprinkle with the vinegar. Dot with slivers of the butter. Roll out the top crust and fit over the pie. Fold the top edge over the bottom to seal and press the edges between your fingers to crimp. Cut slits in the top for escape of steam. Bake in the oven for 10 minutes. Reduce heat to 350°F and bake an additional 35 to 40 minutes, or until the crust is browned and the filling bubbles. Cool on a wire rack.

MAKES 6 TO 8 SERVINGS.

Lemon Sponge Pie

My mother's Lemon Sponge Pie was one of my favorites when I was growing up. Mother never measured her lemon juice when she made it. She just used whatever one lemon provided. If that lemon was large, she threw in a little extra flour to compensate.

Pastry for Single-Crust Pie (page 129)
2 tablespoons unsalted butter, softened
1 cup granulated sugar
3 large eggs, separated
2 tablespoons bleached all-purpose flour
⅛ teaspoon salt
¼ cup fresh lemon juice
Grated zest of 1 lemon
1 cup milk

1. Preheat the oven to 350°F.

2. Roll out pastry. Line a 9-inch pie pan with the pastry. Trim and flute the edges.

3. In a mixing bowl, cream the butter and the sugar with a wooden spoon. Add the egg yolks and beat until smooth. Stir in the flour, salt, lemon juice, and zest. Stir in the milk. In a separate bowl beat the egg whites until stiff, then fold into the batter.

4. Pour into the unbaked pie shell. Bake in the preheated oven for 40 to 45 minutes, or until lightly browned. Cool on a wire rack. Serve slightly warm or at room temperature. Refrigerate leftovers.

MAKES 6 TO 8 SERVINGS.

Velvet Pie

Velvety smooth, with a just-right sweet vanilla flavor, this is a wonderful custard pie.

> *Pastry for a Single-Crust Pie (page 129)*
> *2½ cups milk, scalded*
> *4 large eggs*
> *⅔ cup granulated sugar*
> *¼ teaspoon salt*
> *1½ teaspoons vanilla extract*
> *¼ teaspoon ground nutmeg*

Touring Amish Country

A self-directed tour is the best way to visit an Amish-Mennonite community. On an organized tour, you are constrained to stop only where the tour prescribes. If you head out on your own, you can go as slowly as you wish, enjoying the bucolic atmosphere of the gently farmed countryside, and stop as often as your whims dictate, visiting with and getting to know the gentle people who operate farm-attached businesses and shops.

A call to the local visitors bureau will bring you literature to help you become familiar with the area. Many communities have guidebooks, maps, and audiocassettes to help you plan your tour. For Indiana call 800-254-8090; for Pennsylvania dial 800-324-1518; for Ohio call 800-282-5393; for Kansas call 800-899-0455; for Illinois call 800-722-6474.

While touring, keep two things in mind. Amish people, in keeping with their religious beliefs, prefer not to be photographed and horse-drawn vehicles travel more slowly than cars. Drive carefully, especially when cresting a hill. You may find you enjoy a day in which speed has no importance.

1. Preheat the oven to 450°F.

2. Roll out pastry. Line a 9-inch pie pan with the pastry. Crimp and make a high fluted edge (to contain all the filling). Chill the shell while preparing the filling.

3. Scald the milk first so it can partially cool while you are preparing the rest of the filling. In a mixing bowl beat the eggs with a wire whisk just until smooth. Do not overbeat, as you want to avoid beating in air. Add the sugar and salt and beat again just until smooth. Switch to a metal spoon and gradually stir in the milk. Stir in the vanilla.

4. Pour the filling into the chilled pie shell. Sprinkle the nutmeg over the top. Place the pie in the oven, taking care not to tilt it. Bake in the oven for 10 minutes. Reduce the heat to 325°F and continue to bake for 30 to 40 minutes longer, or until a knife inserted halfway between the center and the edge comes out clean. Cool on a wire rack. Serve at room temperature or chilled. Be sure to refrigerate any leftovers.

MAKES 6 SERVINGS.

Poppy Seed Pie

This wonderful pie comes from the Mennonites who lived for a time in Russia before migrating to the United States. The pie filling is a creamy custard, flavored and textured with deep blue-black poppy seeds.

Pastry for a Single-Crust Pie (page 129)
¾ cup granulated sugar
2 tablespoons cornstarch
2 large eggs
2 cups heavy (whipping) cream
2 ounces (scant ½ cup) poppy seeds
1 teaspoon vanilla extract

1. Roll out pastry. Line a 9-inch pie pan with the pastry to form a pie shell. Prick the dough generously with a fork all over the bottom

and sides. Gently line the shell with regular-weight aluminum foil to keep the shell from losing shape. Bake in a preheated 425°F oven for 6 minutes. Remove the foil. Bake for 7 to 9 minutes longer, or until lightly browned. Set aside to cool while making filling.

2. In a medium saucepan stir together the sugar and the cornstarch. Add the eggs and beat with a metal spoon until smooth. Slowly and gently stir in the cream. Stir in the poppy seeds. Cook over medium to medium-high heat, stirring constantly, until the mixture thickens, 5 to 7 minutes. Remove from heat. Stir in the vanilla. Pour into the baked pie shell. Chill to firm. Serve as is or with a dollop of whipped cream. Be sure to refrigerate leftovers.

MAKES 6 TO 8 SERVINGS.

Apple Butter Pie

After making jar after jar of apple butter, the ingenious Amish-Mennonite cook thinks of ways to use it all. One delightful result is this satisfying custard pie.

2 large eggs
½ cup granulated sugar
⅛ teaspoon salt
½ teaspoon ground cinnamon
¼ teaspoon ground nutmeg
1 cup apple butter
1 can (12 ounces) evaporated milk
Pastry for a Single-Crust Pie (page 129)

1. Preheat the oven to 400°F.

2. In a mixing bowl, beat the eggs with a metal spoon until smooth. In a small bowl, stir the sugar, salt, cinnamon, and nutmeg together, then stir this mixture into the eggs. Stir in the apple butter. Slowly and gently stir in the evaporated milk. Roll out pastry. Line a 9-inch pie pan with the pastry to form a pie shell. Pour the filling mixture into the pie shell and bake in the oven for 35 to 40 minutes, or until the pie is set

in the center. Cool on a wire rack. Serve at room temperature or chilled. Be sure to refrigerate leftovers.

MAKES 6 TO 8 SERVINGS.

Union Pie

Despite its name, this pie has nothing to do with the War Between the States. The name refers to the union of the ingredients used. Some say it's the union of the sour cream with the buttermilk; others, the union of the sweet flavors of the sugar and the syrup with the sour flavors of the sour cream and the buttermilk. Whichever it is, the combination makes for a very tasty pie.

½ cup granulated sugar
1 tablespoon bleached all-purpose flour
¼ teaspoon baking soda
¼ teaspoon ground cinnamon
¼ teaspoon ground nutmeg
1 large egg
½ cup light corn syrup
½ cup sour cream
½ cup buttermilk
Pastry for a Single-Crust Pie (page 129)

1. Preheat the oven to 400°F.

2. In a medium-size bowl stir together the sugar, flour, baking soda, cinnamon, and nutmeg. Add the egg and beat with a metal spoon until smooth. Add the corn syrup, sour cream, and buttermilk one at a time, blending well after each. Roll out pastry. Line a 9-inch pie pan with the pastry to form a pie shell. Pour the filling into the pie shell. Bake in the oven at 400°F for 10 minutes. Reduce the heat to 325°F and bake for 20 to 25 minutes longer, or until a knife inserted in the center comes out clean. The pie will poof up as it bakes, then deflate as it cools. Cool on a wire rack. Refrigerate leftovers.

MAKES 6 TO 8 SERVINGS.

Vinegar Pie

What do you do when lemons are scarce? You make vinegar pie. Try it—you'll be surprised.

> *Pastry for a Single-Crust Pie (page 129)*
> *1 cup granulated sugar*
> *⅓ cup bleached all-purpose flour*
> *Pinch salt*
> *¼ cup cider vinegar*
> *1¼ cups boiling water*
> *1 tablespoon unsalted butter, softened*
> *1 large egg*

1. Preheat the oven to 350°F.

2. Roll out pastry. Line a 9-inch pie pan with the pastry. Make a high fluted edge.

3. In a medium-size saucepan, stir together the sugar, flour, and salt. Stir in the vinegar, then the boiling water. Cook over medium heat, stirring constantly, until thickened, 1 to 2 minutes. Remove from the heat. Stir in the butter until melted.

4. In a measuring cup, beat the egg with a fork until smooth. Adding 1 spoonful at a time, stir about ½ cup of the hot vinegar mixture into the egg. Stir the egg mixture back into the remaining vinegar mixture. Pour the filling into the pie shell. Bake in the oven for 35 minutes or until the filling is set. Cool on a wire rack. Serve at room temperature or chilled. Be sure to refrigerate leftovers.

MAKES 6 TO 8 SERVINGS.

Gravel Pie

Amish and Mennonite cooks use crumb mixtures in many of their recipes. This intriguing pie consists of the crumbs alone baked in a crust. Leftovers are enjoyed at breakfast sliced thinly, dunked into milk-laced coffee.

Pastry for a Single-Crust Pie (page 129)
1½ cups bleached all-purpose flour
1 cup light brown sugar, firmly packed
1 teaspoon ground cinnamon
½ teaspoon salt
½ cup (1 stick) unsalted butter, softened
½ cup finely chopped pecans

1. Preheat the oven to 350°F.

2. Roll out the pastry. Line a 9-inch pie pan with the pastry. Trim and flute the edges.

3. Mix the flour, sugar, cinnamon, and salt together. Cut in the butter to make fine crumbs. Add the pecans and toss lightly with a fork to mix. Spoon lightly into the pastry-lined pan.

4. Bake in the preheated oven for 30 to 35 minutes, or until lightly browned. Cool on a wire rack.

MAKES 8 SERVINGS.

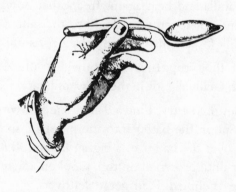

Funny-Cake Pie

The layers of this pie reverse in baking. The syrup that is poured on top becomes a chocolate pudding on the bottom; the batter rises as it bakes to form a golden cakelike top.

CAKE
¼ cup (½ stick) unsalted butter, softened
1 cup granulated sugar
1 large egg
½ teaspoon vanilla extract
1 cup bleached all-purpose flour
1 teaspoon baking powder
Pinch salt
½ cup milk

SYRUP
½ cup granulated sugar
4 tablespoons unsweetened cocoa powder
⅓ cup plus 1 tablespoon cool water
½ teaspoon vanilla extract

Pastry for a Single-Crust Pie (page 129)

1. Preheat the oven to 350°F.

2. Prepare the cake layer: In a mixing bowl, beat the butter and 1 cup sugar with a wooden spoon until light and fluffy. Add the egg and the ½ teaspoon vanilla and beat again. In another bowl stir the flour, baking powder, and salt together and add to the butter mixture alternately with the milk (3 parts dry ingredients, 2 parts milk).

3. Prepare the syrup: In a small bowl, stir the ½ cup sugar and the cocoa together. Gradually stir in the water and the ½ teaspoon vanilla.

4. Roll out the pastry. Line a 9-inch pie pan with the pastry to form a pie shell. Spoon the batter into the pie shell, spreading evenly. Drizzle the syrup over the batter in a zigzag fashion. Bake in the oven for 40 minutes, or until browned on top. Cool on a wire rack. Serve at room temperature or chilled. Refrigerate leftovers.

MAKES 6 TO 8 SERVINGS.

Pennsylvania Dutch Shoofly Pie

Recent recipes for Shoofly Pie include cinnamon and nutmeg. Earlier versions do not, letting the pure molasses flavor steal the show. I list the spices as optional, so that you can try it either way.

Pastry for a Single-Crust Pie (page 129)

CRUMB TOPPING
1 cup bleached all-purpose flour
⅔ cup light brown sugar, firmly packed
½ teaspoon ground cinnamon, optional
⅛ teaspoon ground nutmeg, optional
6 tablespoons unsalted butter, cut into 6 pieces

SYRUP
1 cup unsulphured molasses
1 cup boiling water
⅛ teaspoon salt
1 teaspoon baking soda

1. Preheat the oven to 375°F.

2. Roll out the pastry. Line a 9-inch pie pan with the pastry to form a pie shell. Refrigerate the unbaked pie shell to chill while preparing the pie.

3. Prepare the crumb topping: In a food processor, process the flour, sugar, cinnamon, and nutmeg to mix. Add the butter and process to make fine crumbs. (Alternately, stir the flour, sugar, and spices together in a mixing bowl. Cut in the butter with a pastry blender.)

4. Prepare the syrup: In a small bowl stir together the molasses, ½ cup of the boiling water, and the salt. In a separate bowl stir together the remaining boiling water and baking soda, then stir this into the molasses mixture. Spread 1 cup of the crumbs in an even layer in the pie shell. Gently pour the syrup over the crumbs. Sprinkle the remaining crumbs evenly on top. Bake in the oven for 30 to 35 minutes, or until the crumb topping is browned. Cool on a wire rack. Serve at room temperature or chilled. Refrigerate leftovers.

MAKES 6 TO 8 SERVINGS.

Amish Vanilla Pie

This is similar to the Pennsylvania Dutch Shoofly Pie, but the flavor is much milder, using vanilla rather than molasses and the usual spices.

CRUMBS
1 cup bleached all-purpose flour
½ cup light brown sugar, firmly packed
½ teaspoon baking soda
½ teaspoon baking powder
5 tablespoons unsalted butter, cut into 6 pieces

SYRUP
½ cup light brown sugar
½ cup light corn syrup
1 tablespoon bleached all-purpose flour
1 large egg
1 cup hot water
1½ teaspoons vanilla extract

Pastry for a Single-Crust Pie (page 129)

1. Preheat the oven to 375°F.

2. Prepare the crumbs: In a food processor, process the 1 cup flour, ½ cup light brown sugar, baking soda, and baking powder just long enough to mix. Add the butter and process to make fine crumbs. (Alternately, stir the dry ingredients together in a mixing bowl and then cut the butter in with a pastry blender.) Set aside.

3. Prepare the pie: In a medium saucepan, stir together the ½ cup brown sugar, corn syrup, 1 tablespoon flour, and the egg until smooth. Stir in the water and vanilla. Cook over medium heat, stirring constantly, until thickened to the consistency of thin gravy, 3 to 5 minutes. Roll out pastry. Line a 9-inch pie pan with the pastry to form a pie shell. Pour the syrup mixture into the pie shell. Sprinkle the reserved crumbs over the top. Bake in the oven for 35 to 40 minutes, or until the crumbs are lightly browned. Cool on a wire rack. Serve slightly warm, at room temperature, or chilled. Be sure to refrigerate leftovers.

MAKES 6 TO 8 SERVINGS.

Collage Pie

This recipe makes two pies with a thick syrupy base and a cakelike top. The cake batter is dropped into the pie shell and the syrup is poured over it. In the baking, the batter rises through the syrup to form the cake topping. The combination of cinnamon and molasses gives it come-back-for-more flavor.

SYRUP
1 cup light brown sugar, firmly packed
1 tablespoon bleached all-purpose flour
⅛ teaspoon salt
1 large egg
½ cup unsulphured molasses
2 cups hot water
1 teaspoon vanilla extract

CAKE BATTER
¼ cup white vegetable shortening
1 cup granulated sugar
1 large egg
½ cup sour cream
1 cup bleached all-purpose flour
1 teaspoon ground cinnamon
¼ teaspoon salt
¼ teaspoon baking powder
¼ teaspoon baking soda

Pastry for 2 Single-Crust Pies (double recipe, page 129)

1. Preheat the oven to 350°F.

2. Prepare the syrup: In a medium saucepan stir together the brown sugar, 1 tablespoon flour, and ⅛ teaspoon salt. Add 1 egg and beat with a metal spoon until the dry ingredients are wet. Add the molasses and beat until smooth. Gradually stir in the water. Stir in the vanilla. Cook over medium-high heat, stirring constantly, until the mixture thickens slightly, 3 to 5 minutes. Remove from heat and reserve.

3. Prepare the cake batter: In a mixing bowl beat the shortening and granulated sugar together until well mixed. Add the 1 egg and beat again. Stir in the sour cream. In a separate bowl sift or whisk together the 1 cup flour, cinnamon, ¼ teaspoon salt, baking powder, and baking soda, then stir this mixture into the sour cream mixture.

4. Roll out pastry. Line two 9-inch pie pans with the pastry to form 2 pie shells. Drop rounded tablespoonfuls of the batter into the pie shells, dividing the batter evenly between them. (I put 1 spoonful in the center of each pie shell and surround that with a circle of 6 more spoonfuls.) Pour the syrup over the batter, dividing the syrup evenly between the 2 pie shells. Bake in the oven for 40 minutes, or until the tops of the pies and the edges of the crusts are browned. Cool on a wire rack. Serve just slightly warm, at room temperature, or chilled. Be sure to refrigerate leftovers.

MAKES 12 TO 16 SERVINGS.

Half-Moon Pies

These little pies were designed as a good dessert to carry in a lunch box to be eaten out of your hand, no matter where you were. The pastry is so light and flaky, however, that I recommend positioning the pie on the safety of a plate to be enjoyed with the aid of a fork.

PASTRY
3 cups bleached all-purpose flour
1 teaspoon salt
1¼ cups white vegetable shortening
1 large egg
⅓ cup cool water
1 tablespoon cider vinegar

FILLING
1 pound dried apricots (about 3 cups)
1 cup cool water
1 teaspoon fresh lemon juice

½ cup granulated sugar
½ cup light brown sugar, firmly packed
½ teaspoon ground cinnamon
½ teaspoon ground allspice
Pinch salt

FROSTING
1 cup powdered sugar
½ teaspoon vanilla extract
2 to 3 tablespoons hot water

1. Preheat the oven to 400°F.

2. Prepare the pastry: In a medium-size bowl, stir together the flour and the 1 teaspoon salt. With a pastry blender, cut in the shortening until only small lumps remain. In a measuring cup, beat the egg, ⅓ cup water, and vinegar together with a fork until smooth. Add to the dry ingredients and stir with a fork just until the dough comes together. Divide the dough in half. Gently pat each half into a ball. Cover the pastry with plastic wrap and chill while making the filling.

3. Prepare the filling: Place the apricots, 1 cup of water, and lemon juice in a covered heavy saucepan and simmer for about 20 minutes, or until almost all the liquid has been absorbed by the fruit. Drain the apricots. In a mixing bowl, stir together the sugars, spices, and pinch of salt. Add the drained apricots and mix well.

4. On a lightly floured surface, roll out one ball of the pastry dough to slightly larger than a 10 × 15-inch rectangle. Cut out 6 5-inch circles of the dough and transfer to an ungreased baking sheet. (I use a 5-inch diameter pan lid. If you lack one the right size, cut a 5-inch circle out of cardboard to use as a guide.) Spoon two rounded tablespoons of filling onto each circle, placing the filling slightly off center. Lift and fold the dough in half to cover the filling, and press the edges together firmly with your fingertips to seal. Cut a 1-inch gash in the top of each pie. Bake for 20 to 25 minutes, or until the pastry is very lightly browned. Transfer to wire racks to cool. Repeat with the remaining ball of dough. While the pies are still slightly warm, prepare the frosting.

5. Prepare the frosting: In a small bowl stir together the powdered sugar, vanilla, and 2 to 3 tablespoons of water. Drizzle frosting over the half-moon pies. If you have pastry dough left over, use to make Pie Crust Cookies (page 74). If you have filling left over, use as breakfast jam.

MAKES 12 HALF-MOON PIES.

Cookie Jar
Favorites

My grandmothers kept their cookie jars full, my mother did the same, and I have tried to follow suit. When your children are home, and later in life when your grandchildren come to visit, it's a homemade cookie that tastes good with a glass of milk. Much preferred over something store-bought, don't you think?

If you want something easy, try the Chewy Oatmeal Cookies, Michigan Rocks, *Grossmutter*'s Cookies, or Chocolate Drops. If you like a frosted cookie, there are Brown Sugar Drops and Soft Molasses Cookies. For a reliable cut-out cookie, make Relief Sale Sugar Cookies. At Christmas time, surprise your family with Pfeffernüsse and Zuckernüsse. For something unusual, try Whoopie Pies. And when making pie crusts, don't forget to make Pie Crust Cookies.

Grossmutter's Cookies

When you travel the back roads in Amish country, you may notice clusters of buildings at an Amish farmstead. Often as not, there will be two homes, one smaller than the other. When a son marries, the small house is provided for the newlyweds. As the family develops, the son may trade houses with the parents, so that the younger family has more room to grow. What better way to get the grandchildren to come to *Grossmutter*'s house to visit than to keep the cookie jar filled with these soft, cakelike cookies?

1 cup white vegetable shortening
1 cup granulated sugar
1 cup light brown sugar, firmly packed
2 large eggs
1 tablespoon vanilla extract
3 cups bleached all-purpose flour
½ teaspoon salt
1 teaspoon baking powder
1 teaspoon baking soda
1 cup buttermilk

1. Preheat the oven to 350°F. Lightly grease 2 baking sheets, or use nonstick.

2. Place the shortening in a large mixing bowl. Gradually add the granulated sugar, beating well with a wooden spoon. Add the brown sugar and beat again. Add the eggs, one at a time, beating well after each. Stir in the vanilla.

3. Sift the flour, salt, baking powder, and baking soda together and then add to the creamed sugar mixture alternately with the buttermilk (3 parts flour mixture, 2 parts buttermilk).

4. Drop by rounded teaspoonfuls onto baking sheets, spacing drops 2 inches apart. Bake in the oven for about 12 minutes. The bottoms of the cookies should brown, but the tops should not. Transfer to wire racks to cool.

MAKES 6 DOZEN 2½-INCH COOKIES.

Brown Sugar Drops

The sour cream in these cookies makes them chewy-tender. The brown sugar in the frosting gives them a caramel-like coating. Scrumptious!

COOKIES
½ cup white vegetable shortening
1 cup light brown sugar, firmly packed
1 large egg

¼ cup sour cream
1¾ cups bleached all-purpose flour
½ teaspoon salt
½ teaspoon baking soda

FROSTING
6 tablespoons light brown sugar
3 tablespoons unsalted butter, softened
3 tablespoons sour cream
Pinch salt
About 1½ cups powered sugar

Are All Amish Alike?

There are many varieties of Amish. To the outsider, these can be evidenced by changes in dress style or in the design of the buggies owned by the members of one sect or another. Change in accepted practices and styles can happen over time but are not brought about by individual whim. If a change is made, it is after consideration by the leaders of an individual church. Conformity to accepted styles is enforced by a practice called "shunning." If an individual decides on his own to defy the elders of the church, the rest of the community shuns that person. He is not spoken to, and no one sits at his table when he eats. When the individual recants his actions, he is forgiven and taken back into the fold.

One practice that is the same for all Amish is that of holding church in their homes. This dates back to the 1500s when Anabaptist followers were severely persecuted if found meeting for worship. To avoid detection, they met in homes, changing the meeting location every week, so that it looked as though they were simply visiting. Although they now have religious freedom, the Amish continue to meet in homes, usually every other week. A special "church wagon" carries backless wooden benches from farm to farm for the services that can last as long as four hours. After church, lunch is served with home-baked breads, pies, cakes, and cookies as part of the meal.

1. Preheat the oven to 375°F.

2. Prepare the cookies: In a mixing bowl beat the shortening and 1 cup brown sugar with a wooden spoon until smooth. Add the egg and beat again. Stir in the ¼ cup sour cream. In a smaller mixing bowl sift or whisk together the flour, ½ teaspoon salt, and baking soda. Stir the flour mixture into the dough. Drop by rounded teaspoonfuls onto ungreased baking sheets. Bake in the oven for 8 to 10 minutes, or until lightly browned. Cool on wire racks.

3. While the cookies are cooling, prepare the frosting: In a small saucepan, stir the 6 tablespoons brown sugar, butter, 3 tablespoons sour cream, and pinch of salt over medium heat until the butter is melted and the mixture bubbles. Remove from heat. Stir in enough of the powdered sugar to make the mixture spreadable. Spread on the cooled cookies.

MAKES 3 DOZEN 2-INCH COOKIES.

Michigan Rocks

My mother and father argued about a lot of things, including the name for these cookies. Dad, who spent part of his growing-up years in Michigan, insisted they be called Michigan Rocks. Mom said that was silly and simply called them Rocks. As usual, I sided with Dad.

1 cup white vegetable shortening
¾ cup granulated sugar
¾ cup light brown sugar, firmly packed
3 large eggs
1 tablespoon strong brewed coffee
3 cups bleached all-purpose flour
1 teaspoon salt
1 teaspoon baking soda
1 teaspoon ground cinnamon
1 teaspoon ground ginger
1 teaspoon ground nutmeg
1 teaspoon ground allspice

1 cup raisins
1 cup chopped dates
1 cup chopped dried apricots
1 cup chopped walnuts

1. Preheat the oven to 350°F. Lightly grease 2 baking sheets, or use nonstick.

2. In a mixing bowl beat the shortening and the sugars with a wooden spoon until light and fluffy. Add the eggs and beat again. Stir in the coffee. Sift or whisk together in a bowl the flour, salt, baking soda, cinnamon, ginger, nutmeg, and allspice, then stir this mixture into the dough. Mix in the fruit and nuts.

3. Drop by rounded teaspoonfuls on the baking sheets and bake for 12 to 15 minutes, or until lightly browned. Cool on wire racks.
MAKES 6 DOZEN 1¾-INCH COOKIES.

Chewy Oatmeal Cookies

These cookies are big enough to be worth pouring a glass of milk for— a full three inches of chewy goodness filled with plump raisins and good-for-you oatmeal.

1 cup raisins
½ cup water
¾ cup white vegetable shortening
¾ cup granulated sugar
¾ cup light brown sugar, firmly packed
2 large eggs
1 teaspoon vanilla extract
2 cups bleached all-purpose flour
½ teaspoon salt
1 teaspoon baking soda
1 teaspoon ground cinnamon
3 cups uncooked old-fashioned or quick oatmeal (not instant)

1. Preheat oven to 350°F.

2. In a small saucepan combine the raisins and water. Boil for 1 minute over high heat. Remove from heat.

3. In a mixing bowl beat the shortening and granulated sugar with a wooden spoon. Add the brown sugar and beat again. Add the eggs, 1 at a time, beating well after each. Stir in the vanilla.

4. Drain the raisins, reserving the liquid.

5. Sift or whisk together in a mixing bowl the flour, salt, baking soda, and cinnamon. Mix ½ of the dry ingredients into the dough. Add ¼ cup of the reserved raisin liquid and mix. Mix in the remaining dry ingredients. Stir in the raisins. Stir in the oatmeal.

6. Drop rounded tablespoonfuls of the dough onto ungreased baking sheets, allowing ample space for spread. (I place 8 drops of dough per sheet.) Bake in the oven for about 12 minutes, or until lightly browned on top. Transfer to wire racks to cool.

MAKES 3 DOZEN 3-INCH COOKIES.

Chocolate Drops

Ever since I started putting chocolate chips in my chocolate drops, my family complains that we run out of the cookies much too fast. I have devised this big-batch recipe to keep everyone happy.

1 cup white vegetable shortening
2 cups granulated sugar
1 tablespoon vanilla extract
4 large eggs
3 cups bleached all-purpose flour
1 teaspoon salt
1½ teaspoons baking powder
1 teaspoon baking soda
1 cup unsweetened cocoa powder
1 cup milk
4 cups (24 ounces) semisweet chocolate morsels

1. Preheat the oven to 375°F. Lightly grease 2 baking sheets, or use nonstick.

2. In a mixing bowl beat the shortening and sugar with a wooden spoon until soft and fluffy. Add the vanilla and the eggs and beat again. Sift or whisk together in a separate bowl the flour, salt, baking powder, baking soda, and cocoa. Add to the batter alternately with the milk (4 parts dry ingredients, 3 parts milk). Stir in the chocolate morsels.

3. Drop the dough by well-rounded teaspoonfuls onto the baking sheets, leaving 2 to 3 inches between drops. Bake for 10 to 12 minutes, or until the top of one of the cookies springs back when lightly touched in the center. They should not brown. Cool on wire racks.

MAKES 8 DOZEN 2½-INCH COOKIES.

Soft Molasses Cookies

The formula for soft molasses cookies may vary from kitchen to kitchen, but it is the rare Amish-Mennonite baker who does not hail at least one as a specialty. These are soft and gingery and are frosted with a butter cream that is flavored with both lemon and orange. The combination is absolutely perfect.

COOKIES
½ cup white vegetable shortening
1 cup granulated sugar
1 large egg
4 cups bleached all-purpose flour
1 teaspoon salt
2 teaspoons baking soda
2 teaspoons ground ginger
1 teaspoon ground cinnamon
1 teaspoon ground nutmeg
1 teaspoon ground cloves
1 cup molasses
1 cup boiling water

FROSTING
3¾ cups (1 pound) powdered sugar
2 tablespoons unsalted butter, softened
1 teaspoon lemon extract
1 teaspoon orange extract
4 to 6 tablespoons milk

1. Preheat the oven to 375°F. Lightly grease two baking sheets, or use nonstick.

2. Prepare the cookies: In a mixing bowl, cream the shortening and granulated sugar with a wooden spoon. Add the egg and beat well.

3. Sift or whisk together in another mixing bowl the flour, salt, baking soda, ginger, cinnamon, nutmeg, and cloves. In another bowl mix the molasses with the boiling water. Add the flour mixture to the batter alternately with the molasses mixture.

4. Drop by rounded teaspoonfuls onto the baking sheets, leaving 1½ inches between drops. Keep unused batter covered to prevent drying out. Bake in the oven until the cookies are set but not browned, 8 to 10 minutes. Cool on wire racks.

5. Prepare the frosting: Mix together the powdered sugar, butter, and extracts. Add enough milk to make a spreadable consistency. Spread a thin layer of frosting on the top of each cooled cookie.
MAKES 6 DOZEN 2-INCH COOKIES.

Sour Cream Cookies

These have a delicate texture and a wonderful sour cream flavor. The dough is almost too soft to handle, but there's a little trick to shaping them without getting "sticky" everywhere. Here's how. Dip cookie dough out of the bowl with a spoon; use your left hand to push the gobs of dough off the spoon into the sugar they are to be rolled in; use your right hand to toss them in the sugar and retrieve and place them on the baking sheet. Reverse these actions if you are left-handed, of course.

½ *cup white vegetable shortening*
1½ *cups granulated sugar*
1 *large egg*
1 *teaspoon vanilla extract*
2 *cups bleached all-purpose flour*
¼ *teaspoon salt*
½ *teaspoon baking soda*
2 *teaspoons baking powder*
½ *cup sour cream*

1. Preheat the oven to 350°F. Use ungreased baking sheets.

2. In a mixing bowl beat the shortening and 1 cup of the sugar with a wooden spoon until creamy. Add the egg and the vanilla and beat until smooth. In another bowl sift or whisk together the flour, salt, baking soda, and baking powder. Stir ½ of the sour cream into the dough, then ½ of the dry ingredients. Repeat. Place the remaining ½ cup sugar in a small bowl. Drop a rounded teaspoonful of the dough into the sugar. Toss to coat the ball of dough evenly with the sugar. Take care not to compact the ball of dough. The ball should end up being about 1¼-inches in diameter.

3. Transfer the cookie ball to the baking sheet. Repeat, spacing the cookies about 2 inches apart. Bake in the oven for 10 to 12 minutes, or until lightly browned. Transfer to wire racks to cool.
MAKES 4 DOZEN 2¼-INCH COOKIES.

Relief Sale Sugar Cookies

When you attend a Mennonite relief sale (see schedule on page 69), you will find wonderful baked goods for sale. The church women of the area will have selected one or more recipes that all will make to sell. You may find homemade cinnamon rolls, tea rings, yeast-risen doughnuts, or cookies like these. I find the beauty of these sugar cookies is that they can be made a day ahead and are easy to stack and carry—and the flavor of the cookie is even better the second day!

½ cup (1 stick) unsalted butter, softened
½ cup white vegetable shortening
1 cup granulated sugar
1 cup light brown sugar, firmly packed
1 tablespoon vanilla extract
2 large eggs
½ teaspoon salt
1 tablespoon baking powder
4 cups bleached all-purpose flour
¼ cup milk

Mennonite Relief Sales

Mennonite relief sales are a grassroots phenomenon. The first such sale is said to have been held in Gap, Pennsylvania, in 1957. Since that beginning, sales have developed in communities all over the United States and Canada. Although each sale is unique, there are unifying characteristics in the abundance of good food and the reasonably priced handcrafted goods available. One sale I attended featured oversized yeast-risen doughnuts and enticingly sweet cinnamon rolls. Another year there might be frosted and decorated tea rings (actually made of cinnamon rolls laid end to end, then joined to form a circle), gigantic sugar cookies, and homemade egg noodles. There are wonderful bargains to be found in the auctions and in sale tents. Auctions may feature live farm animals, handcrafted furniture, and beautiful handmade quilts. Proceeds from all North American sales are donated directly to the Mennonite Central Committee for their work in relieving hunger and need throughout the world. If you are interested in attending a sale, here is a partial list (for exact dates and places and a complete listing for the current year, contact the Mennonite Central Committee, 21 South 12th Street, P.O. Box 500, Akron, PA 17501-0500, 717-859-1151):

March	2nd weekend	Lancaster, PA
	3rd weekend	Peoria, IL

1. In a mixing bowl beat the butter and the shortening with a wooden spoon until soft and fluffy. Add the sugars and beat again. Add the vanilla and the eggs and beat again. Add the salt, baking powder, and half of the flour and then stir well to mix. Stir in the milk, then the remaining flour. Cover and chill for 6 hours or overnight to firm the dough.

2. When ready to bake, preheat the oven to 375°F. Lightly grease 2 baking sheets, or use nonstick. Divide the dough into 4 parts. Working with one part at a time (keep unused dough covered and chilled) roll out on a lightly floured surface to slightly less than ¼-inch thickness. Cut out cookies with a 3-inch round cookie cutter.

	last weekend	Harrisburg, PA
		Minot, ND
April	1st weekend	Fresno, CA
		Hutchinson, KS
May	Memorial Day weekend	Iowa City, IA
July	4th weekend	Sioux Falls, SD
August	1st weekend	Fairview, MI
		Kidron, OH
	2nd weekend	Gap, PA
		Jefferson, WI
	4th weekend	Arthur, IL
September	2nd weekend	Montgomery, IN
	3rd weekend	Goshen, IN
	last weekend	Fisherville, VA
		Albany, OR
October	1st weekend	Ritzville, WA
	2nd weekend	Harrisonville, MO
	3rd weekend	Rocky Ford, CO
	4th weekend	Johnstown, PA
November	1st weekend	Houston, TX
	Thanksgiving weekend	Fairview, OK

3. Place the cutouts on the baking sheets, leaving 1 inch space between each. Bake for 8 to 10 minutes, or until lightly browned. Transfer to wire racks to cool.

MAKES 4 DOZEN 3-INCH COOKIES.

Pfeffernüsse, or Peppernuts

Pfeffernüsse are a Christmas specialty in many Mennonite kitchens. They keep well and can be made early in the season. In fact, they should be made at least one day ahead of serving to let the anise and other spice flavors develop. Their tiny size invites snacking while you wrap presents or decorate the tree.

Although some cooks roll their *pfeffernüsse* dough into tiny little balls, it is much easier to slice them from a refrigerated roll as I suggest here.

¾ cup (1½ sticks) unsalted butter, softened
¾ cup light brown sugar, firmly packed
¾ cup molasses
1 large egg
4 cups bleached all-purpose flour
½ teaspoon baking soda
½ teaspoon salt
½ teaspoon ground cinnamon
½ teaspoon ground cloves
½ teaspoon ground mace
½ teaspoon ground white pepper
½ teaspoon aniseeds, crushed or chopped

1. In a mixing bowl cream the butter and brown sugar. Blend in the molasses and then the egg. In another bowl whisk the remaining ingredients together. Stir into the butter mixture 1 cup at a time.

2. Divide the dough into 6 parts. Shape each part into a 1-inch-diameter roll, about 8 inches long. Wrap tightly in waxed paper and refrigerate to chill for at least 4 hours.

3. Preheat the oven to 350°F. Lightly grease a baking sheet or use nonstick.

4. Slice the dough rolls into ¼-inch-thick slices and place one inch apart on baking sheets. Bake in the preheated oven for 9 minutes, or until lightly browned on the bottom. Transfer to wire racks to cool. MAKES 16 DOZEN 1¼-INCH *PFEFFERNÜSSE*.

Zuckernüsse, or Sugarnuts

Zuckernüsse are not as common in Amish-Mennonite baking literature as *pfeffernüsse*, perhaps because of a lack of spice. I find their soft almond sweetness, however, to be a nice contrast to the spice of the other cookies that I make for the Christmas season.

> 1 cup unsalted butter, softened
> 1 cup granulated sugar
> ½ teaspoon almond extract
> ½ teaspoon vanilla extract
> 2 cups bleached all-purpose flour
> 2 tablespoons cornstarch
> ⅛ teaspoon salt

1. In a mixing bowl beat the butter until soft and fluffy. Add ½ cup of the sugar and beat again. Blend in the extracts. In a smaller bowl sift or whisk together the flour with the cornstarch and salt. Stir 1 cup of this mixture into the dough. Add the remaining flour mixture, ¼ cup at a time. If you cannot stir all the flour in with a spoon, use your hands. Gather the dough up into a ball and return to bowl. Cover and chill for 1 hour.

2. When ready to bake, preheat the oven to 325°F. Lightly grease two baking sheets, or use nonstick. Place the remaining ½ cup of sugar in a small bowl. Divide the dough into four parts. Working with one part at a time (keep remaining dough covered and chilled), roll the dough with your hands on a lightly floured surface to a 6-inch-long log. Slice

the log into ½-inch-thick slices. Roll the slices between your palms to form balls. Roll the balls in the bowl of sugar to coat.

3. Place balls on a baking sheet, leaving 2 inches between balls. Bake in the oven for about 15 to 18 minutes, or until set but not browned. They should remain pale. Transfer to wire racks to cool.

MAKES 4 DOZEN 1½-INCH COOKIES.

Whoopee Pies

Whoopee Pies are a specialty of the Amish. If you're wondering where the name comes from, the story goes this way. A young mother was making chocolate cakes one day and found that she had cake batter and frosting left over when her cakes were finished. To satisfy her children's afternoon hunger, she spooned the batter onto baking sheets to make little cakes for a treat. The leftover frosting was spooned in between two of the resulting morsels for a cake sandwich. Upon seeing this invention her children exclaimed, "Whoopee!"

The traditional frosting for Whoopee Pies uses uncooked egg whites. Because of my concern about possible salmonella in raw eggs, I have adapted a frosting recipe that does not use them. There are still small bakeries on farms in what is called "Amish country" where you can find the original frosting used. I was told by a young Amish baker that she and her mother used only eggs they could trust, whether buying from the Amish or their English neighbors. (The Amish call those who are non-Amish "the English.")

CAKES

½ *cup white vegetable shortening*

1 *cup granulated sugar*

1 *large egg*

1 *teaspoon vanilla extract*

2 *cups bleached all-purpose flour*

½ *cup unsweetened cocoa powder*

½ *teaspoon salt*

1 teaspoon baking soda
1 teaspoon cream of tartar
1 cup buttermilk

FROSTING
¼ cup bleached all-purpose flour
Pinch salt
¾ cup milk
¾ cup (1½ sticks) unsalted butter, softened
¾ cup granulated sugar
1½ teaspoons vanilla extract

1. Preheat the oven to 375°F. Lightly grease 2 baking sheets, or use nonstick.

2. Prepare the cakes: In a mixing bowl beat the shortening and the 1 cup sugar with a wooden spoon until light and fluffy. Add the egg and beat to blend. Stir in the 1 teaspoon vanilla. In another bowl sift or whisk together the 2 cups flour, cocoa, ½ teaspoon salt, baking soda, and cream of tartar. Add to the batter alternately with the buttermilk (3 parts dry ingredients, 2 parts buttermilk). Using ¼ cup batter at a time, drop six rounds onto one of the baking sheets. Bake in the oven for 12 to 15 minutes, or until the top of one of the cakes springs back when touched lightly in the center. Remove to cool on wire racks. Repeat the baking until all 18 cakes are made.

3. While they are cooling, prepare the frosting: In a small saucepan stir together the ¼ cup flour and the pinch of salt. Add ¼ cup of the milk and stir, mashing any lumps, to make a smooth paste. Gradually stir in the remaining milk. Cook over medium heat until thickened, about 1 minute after the mixture begins to thicken. Remove from heat to cool, stirring now and then as the mixture cools. Meanwhile, in a mixing bowl beat the butter with a wooden spoon until soft and fluffy. Add the ¾ cup sugar, ¼ cup at a time, beating well after each addition. Stir in the 1½ teaspoons vanilla. Add the cooled milk mixture, 1 spoonful at a time, beating vigorously after each addition to produce a light, fluffy frosting.

4. Assemble the whoopee pies: Place a scant ¼ cup of the frosting on the flat side of 9 of the cakes. Cover with the remaining 9 cakes.

Wrap each whoopee pie separately in plastic wrap. Refrigerate to chill and firm. Serve chilled or at room temperature.

MAKES 9 WHOOPEE PIES.

Pie Crust Cookies

On baking day, my mother made cookies not from a special recipe like this but from scraps left over from trimming her pie crusts. She didn't reroll those scraps but used them in whatever shape they were as she rescued them for her tray of cookies.

> *1 cup bleached all-purpose flour*
> *½ teaspoon salt*
> *6 tablespoons white vegetable shortening*
> *2 to 3 tablespoons cool water*
> *Granulated sugar or Cinnamon-Sugar (page 128) for*
>   *sprinkling on the cookies*

1. Preheat the oven to 425°F.

2. In a medium bowl stir the flour and salt together. Cut in the shortening with a pastry blender or two table knives until the texture is like very coarse cornmeal. Add the water, 1 tablespoon at a time, stirring with a fork all the while, just until the dough comes together. Pat the dough gently to form a ball. Flatten the ball in your hands to about ½ inch thickness.

3. On a lightly floured surface, roll the dough to an 11-inch circle. Cut into 1¼ × 3-inch strips. Lay the strips on an ungreased baking sheet. Sprinkle generously with the sugar. Bake in the oven for 8 to 12 minutes, or until lightly browned. Watch these closely. They go from golden to burned in no time. Transfer to a wire rack to cool.

MAKES 18 TO 24 COOKIES.

Comforting
Desserts

These desserts are the kind that will make your family homesick for your cooking when they are away from home.

Dutch Apple Crisp has lemon-sauced apples topped with sweet buttery crumbs. Apple Pudding combines the pleasures of a cake and a pie. Peach Cobbler is made with sweet canned fruit, as it has been for generations. Rhubarb Dessert has a flavoring surprise that is truly delicious. Amish Bread Pudding is topped with a delightful pineapple sauce. And Amish Date Pudding is layered with bananas and cream to make a delectable triflelike dessert.

Amish Bread Pudding

The frugal Amish housewife saves her slightly stale bread to make old-fashioned bread pudding. This one is spiced with allspice instead of the usual nutmeg. I particularly like it with the pineapple sauce.

PUDDING
3 large eggs
3 cups milk, scalded
⅓ cup plus 1 tablespoon granulated sugar
1 teaspoon ground cinnamon
¼ teaspoon ground allspice
2 tablespoons unsalted butter, softened
4 cups cubed day-old white bread
½ cup raisins

SAUCE
½ cup granulated sugar
1½ tablespoons cornstarch
1½ cups pineapple juice
1 tablespoon fresh lemon juice
1 tablespoon unsalted butter, softened

1. Preheat the oven to 350°F.

2. Prepare the pudding: In a mixing bowl beat the eggs with a metal spoon until smooth. Slowly add the scalded milk, stirring all the while. In a small mixing bowl, stir together ⅓ cup of the sugar with the cinnamon and allspice. Add to the milk mixture along with the 2 tablespoons butter. Stir well.

3. Mix the bread cubes with the raisins in an 8 × 8 × 2-inch baking dish. Pour the custard mixture over the bread and raisins and mix well. Sprinkle with the 1 tablespoon sugar. Place the dish in a large pan and fill the pan with hot water until water comes up 1 inch on side of baking dish. Bake in the preheated oven for 1 hour, or until a knife inserted in the center comes out clean. Cool on a wire rack.

4. Prepare the sauce: In a saucepan stir together the ½ cup sugar and the cornstarch. Stir in the pineapple juice. Stir over high heat until the mixture begins to bubble. Turn the heat down to medium and cook for 2 minutes, stirring constantly. Remove from heat. Stir in the lemon juice and the 1 tablespoon butter.

5. Spoon the pudding into serving dishes. Pour some of the sauce over each serving. Serve warm or cold. Refrigerate leftovers.

MAKES 6 SERVINGS.

Apple Pudding

I like to make this delightful pudding when crisp cooking apples are plentiful in the fall. The sweetened apples cook down to a pie-filling consistency. The batter forms a cakelike topping. It can be embellished with whipped cream, but I usually serve it plain.

1 cup granulated sugar
1 teaspoon ground cinnamon
6 tart cooking apples (1½ pounds), peeled, cored, and sliced
1 cup bleached all-purpose flour
1 teaspoon baking powder

⅛ teaspoon salt
¼ cup milk
¼ cup vegetable oil
1 large egg
1 teaspoon vanilla extract

1. Preheat the oven to 350°F.

2. In a medium bowl stir together the sugar and cinnamon. Spoon out ½ cup of this mixture and toss with the apples in an 8-inch square baking dish.

3. To the remainder of the sugar mixture add the flour, baking powder, and salt; stir to mix. In a measuring cup beat together the milk, oil, egg, and vanilla with a fork. Add the milk mixture to the sugar mixture and stir just until smooth.

4. Spoon the batter evenly over the apples in the pan. Gently spread the batter with a spatula, but don't worry if the batter does not touch the edge of the dish or cover all of the apples.

5. Bake in the oven for 30 to 35 minutes, or until the apples are bubbling and the top springs back when lightly touched in the center. Cool in the pan on a wire rack. Serve pudding warm or cold.

MAKES 6 TO 9 SERVINGS.

Dutch Apple Crisp

In this dessert the apples bake in a lemony sauce with a cinnamon-crumb topping over all. The combination is outstanding.

½ cup granulated sugar
1 tablespoon cornstarch
½ cup hot water
1 tablespoon fresh lemon juice
½ cup bleached all-purpose flour
½ cup light brown sugar, firmly packed
½ teaspoon ground cinnamon
⅛ teaspoon salt
4 tablespoons unsalted butter
4 cups peeled, cored, and quartered, thinly sliced apples

1. Preheat the oven to 375°F.

2. In a small saucepan stir together the granulated sugar and the cornstarch. Stir in the hot water. Cook over medium heat, stirring constantly, until the mixture thickens, about 2 minutes after it begins to thicken. Remove from heat. Gently stir in the lemon juice.

3. In a small bowl stir together the flour, brown sugar, cinnamon, and salt. Cut in the butter to make fine crumbs.

4. Prepare the apples and place in an 8 × 8 × 2-inch baking dish.

5. Pour the lemon sauce over the apples. Sprinkle the crumbs over all. Bake in the oven for 35 minutes. Cool on a wire rack. Serve warm or cold.

MAKES 6 TO 9 SERVINGS.

Amish Date Pudding

Although this pudding is perfectly fine cut into squares and topped with whipped cream, a better and more traditional way to serve it is like a trifle. The cakelike pudding is cut into 1-inch cubes and folded into whipped cream along with chunks of fresh banana. Heaven!

CAKE
1 cup chopped dates
1 teaspoon baking soda
1 tablespoon unsalted butter
1 cup boiling water
1 large egg
1 cup granulated sugar
1½ cups bleached all-purpose flour
½ cup chopped walnuts

1 cup heavy (whipping) cream
2 tablespoons powdered sugar
½ teaspoon vanilla extract
2 to 3 ripe bananas, sliced or cut into small chunks

1. Preheat the oven to 350°F. Grease an 8 × 8 × 2-inch pan.

2. Prepare the cake: Place the dates, baking soda, and butter in a small bowl. Pour the boiling water over all and let stand until cooled.

3. Add the remaining cake ingredients, one at a time, mixing well after each. Spoon the batter into the pan. Bake for 30 to 35 minutes, or until the cake begins to shrink from the sides of the pan. Cool in the pan on a wire rack.

4. To serve: With a whisk or mixer, whip the cream to soft peaks. Gently fold in the powdered sugar and the vanilla. Cut the cake into 1-inch cubes and layer with the banana chunks and the whipped cream either in individual serving dishes or in a bowl to offer at the table.

MAKES 6 TO 8 SERVINGS.

Rhubarb Dessert

Here's another ingenious way to use fruit-flavored gelatin (see recipe for Fresh Strawberry Pie, page 35). Although the strawberry used here enhances both the flavor and the rosy-red color of the rhubarb filling, I sometimes substitute lemon-flavored gelatin to emphasize the tartness of the rhubarb instead.

CRUMB CRUST AND TOPPING
1½ cups bleached all-purpose flour
1 cup granulated sugar
8 tablespoons (1 stick) unsalted butter

FILLING
4 cups thinly sliced fresh rhubarb
1 package (3 ounces) strawberry-flavored gelatin

1. Preheat the oven to 375°F.

2. Prepare the crumb crust and topping: Stir together the flour and the sugar. Cut in the butter to make fine crumbs. Place one half (about 2 cups) of the crumbs in an 8 × 8 × 2-inch baking pan. Gently pat into an even layer.

3. Prepare the filling: Spread the rhubarb slices evenly over the crumb layer. Sprinkle the gelatin powder evenly over the rhubarb.

4. Sprinkle the remaining crumbs evenly over all. Bake in the oven for 40 to 45 minutes, or until the filling bubbles and the top is lightly browned. Cool on a wire rack before cutting into serving pieces. Refrigerate leftovers.

MAKES 9 SERVINGS.

Peach Cobbler

My mother and her sister Lydia often made cobblers with home-canned fruits. Since the fruit was sweetened when canned, they needed only to thicken the juices with a little cornstarch before plopping on the biscuit topping. I have tested this with store-bought canned fruit. It works fine as long as you are sure to buy fruit canned in heavy syrup.

FILLING
1 quart home-canned or 1 can (29 ounces) sliced peaches, packed
*   in heavy syrup*
1 tablespoon cornstarch
½ teaspoon ground cinnamon
1 tablespoon fresh lemon juice
½ cup peach preserves
1 tablespoon unsalted butter, softened

BISCUIT TOPPING
1 cup bleached all-purpose flour
1 tablespoon granulated sugar
¼ teaspoon salt
1½ teaspoons baking powder
¼ cup white vegetable shortening
½ cup milk

1. Preheat the oven to 400°F.

2. Prepare the filling: Drain the peaches, reserving the juice. Place the peaches in a 2-quart casserole. In a small saucepan, stir the cornstarch and cinnamon together. Stir in the lemon juice. Gradually stir in the reserved peach juice. Cook over medium-high heat, stirring constantly, until the mixture thickens. Remove from heat. Stir in the preserves and the butter. Pour over the peaches.

3. Prepare the topping: In a small mixing bowl, stir together the flour, sugar, salt, and baking powder. Cut in the shortening until the mixture resembles coarse cornmeal. Add the milk and stir with a fork

just until the dry ingredients are moistened. Drop rounded teaspoonfuls of the topping over the peaches. It's OK if the peaches are not completely covered. Bake in the oven for 22 to 25 minutes, or until the topping is lightly browned. Cool on a wire rack. Serve warm.

MAKES 4 TO 6 SERVINGS.

Our Daily Bread

The first kind of baking I accomplished with any expertise was bread, and making bread remains the process that I find the most satisfying. The act of combining liquids, flour, and yeast to produce a living dough that can fill a bowl to overflowing and then recharge itself to rise to a glorious loaf of bread is something that continues to amaze and please.

I realized when working on this chapter that I had gotten into a rut with much of my bread baking, making the same French-type loaves over and over again. What a joy to revisit billowy Amish Bakery Bread, rich Milk Bread, sweet Cinnamon Bread, delicious Rich Raisin Bread, old-fashioned Potato-Water Bread, hearty Kansas Wheat Bread, earthy *Roggenbrot,* and nostalgic "Bubbat."

Amish Bakery Bread

These soft, billowy loaves of bread are typical of what you will find at a farmstead Amish bakery. The holes poked in the dough before the last rising are, as an Amish baker told me, "to let the air out." The bread smells heavenly while baking.

Although I have developed the recipe for the home kitchen, the sponge and the dough still require a large container to avoid overflow. The bowl I use holds 4½ quarts.

> *1 cup warm water*
> *2 tablespoons active dry yeast*
> *½ cup plus 1 tablespoon granulated sugar*
> *2 cups milk, scalded*
> *½ cup white vegetable shortening*
> *1 tablespoon salt*
> *1 large egg, beaten*
> *Cool water, enough to make 1 cup with the egg*
> *About 10 cups unbleached all-purpose flour*

1. In a 2-cup measuring cup stir together the water, yeast, and 1 tablespoon sugar. Let stand until foamy, 5 to 10 minutes.

2. In a large mixing bowl put the ½ cup sugar, the shortening, and the salt. Pour in the hot milk and stir to dissolve.

3. In a 1-cup measuring cup, beat the egg. Add cool water to make one cup.

4. Stir the egg mixture into the milk mixture. The combined mixture should be lukewarm. Stir in the yeast mixture. Add 5 cups of the flour and beat well to develop the gluten. Cover and let rest for 30 minutes. (Watch this lest it overflow.)

5. Gradually add the remaining flour to make a soft dough. Turn out on a floured surface and knead gently until smooth and elastic, only picking up enough flour to keep the dough from sticking. You want to end up with a dough that is still somewhat soft. Turn into a well-greased bowl, turning the dough once to grease the top. Cover and let rise until doubled, about 1 hour.

6. Punch the dough down. Divide the dough into 3 parts. Shape each part into a loaf and place in well-greased 9 × 5-inch pans. Place the pans of dough in an unlit oven and place a flat pan of hot water below the loaves. Let rise, uncovered, until risen above the tops of the pans, about 1 hour. Leave the pans in the oven, but remove the water. Turn the oven on, set at 350°F. (You do not preheat the oven before baking.) Bake for about 40 minutes, or until the loaves are brown on the bottom as well as the top, and the loaves sound hollow when tapped on the bottom. Remove from the pans to cool on wire racks.

MAKES 3 LOAVES.

Milk Bread, or *Stretzel*

When you have your own cow, you think nothing of putting a quart of milk into a batch of bread. The Mennonite housewife would bake on Saturday to have bread for a week. I don't have room in my oven for all four loaves at once, so I use one fourth of the dough to make rolls that

I shape first. They rise and bake while the three loaves are still rising (see note).

> *1 quart milk, scalded*
> *⅔ cup white vegetable shortening*
> *½ cup plus 1 teaspoon granulated sugar*
> *1 tablespoon salt*
> *½ cup warm water*
> *2 tablespoons active dry yeast*
> *11 to 12 cups unbleached all-purpose flour*

1. In a large mixing bowl, put the shortening, ½ cup of the sugar, and the salt. Pour in the milk and stir to dissolve the shortening.

2. In a large mixing cup, stir together the warm water, yeast, and 1 teaspoon sugar to soften the yeast. Let stand until the milk mixture has cooled to lukewarm.

3. Add the yeast mixture and 6 cups flour to the milk mixture. Beat well with a wooden spoon. Add 2 cups more flour and beat well again. Gradually add the remaining flour, one cup at a time, to make a stiff dough. Turn out on a floured surface and knead until smooth and elastic. Place the dough in a well-greased bowl, turning once to grease the top. Cover and let rise until doubled in bulk, 1 to 1½ hours. Punch the dough down. Divide into 4 parts. Shape each into a loaf and place in well-greased 9 × 5-inch pans. Cover and let rise until doubled in bulk, about 1 hour. Meanwhile, preheat oven to 375°F. Bake for 30 to 35 minutes, or until loaves sound hollow when tapped on the bottom. Remove from the pans to cool on wire racks.

MAKES 4 LOAVES.

Note: If you wish to make rolls with one part of the dough divide ¼ of the dough into 12 equal pieces. Shape into balls by pulling down the edges. Place the balls in well-greased muffin cups. Cover and let rise in a warm place until doubled, 30 to 45 minutes. Meanwhile preheat oven to 400°F. Bake for 15 to 20 minutes, or until browned. Remove from the pan to cool on wire racks.

Cinnamon Bread

Cinnamon bread is a special treat. It's good warm, straight from the oven. The next day, toast slices for breakfast, or use it to make fantastic French toast.

Dough from Milk Bread (pages 88 and 89)
4 tablespoons unsalted butter, melted
1 cup Cinnamon-Sugar (page 128)

1. Grease 4 9 × 5-inch loaf pans. Make the Milk Bread dough. After the first rising, punch the dough down and divide into four parts. Working with one part at a time, roll the dough out on a lightly floured surface to an 8 × 12-inch rectangle. Spread with 1 tablespoon of the melted butter. Spread ¼ cup of the Cinnamon-Sugar over the butter. Starting with an 8-inch side, roll the dough as for jelly roll. Place in one of the prepared pans. Repeat with the remaining dough.

2. Cover and let rise until doubled in bulk, about 1 hour. Meanwhile, preheat oven to 375°F.

3. Bake for 30 to 35 minutes, or until the loaves sound hollow when tapped on the bottom. Remove from the pans to cool on wire racks.

MAKES 4 LOAVES.

Rich Raisin Bread

The raisins in this recipe are sweetened and plumped by soaking them in the scalded milk along with the butter and brown sugar. Notice there are as many raisins, cup for cup, as there is milk.

> *2 cups milk, scalded*
> *5 tablespoons unsalted butter*
> *¼ cup light brown sugar*
> *1½ teaspoons salt*
> *2 cups raisins*
> *¼ cup warm water*
> *1 tablespoon active dry yeast*
> *1 teaspoon granulated sugar*
> *5½ to 6 cups unbleached all-purpose flour*

1. In a large mixing bowl pour the milk over the butter, brown sugar, salt, and raisins. Stir to melt the butter and dissolve the sugar. Let stand to cool until lukewarm. Meanwhile, in a large measuring cup, stir together the warm water, yeast, and granulated sugar.

2. When the milk mixture has cooled, add the yeast and 3 cups of the flour. Beat well with a wooden spoon. Gradually add the remaining flour to make a soft dough. Turn out onto a floured surface and knead until smooth and elastic.

3. Place in an oiled bowl, turning the dough once to oil the top. Cover and let rise until doubled in bulk, about 1 hour. Punch the dough down. Divide in half and shape each half into a loaf. Place in well-greased 9 × 5-inch pans. Cover and let rise until doubled, about 1 hour.

4. Meanwhile, preheat the oven to 375°F. Bake the loaves in the oven for 35 to 40 minutes, or until the loaves sound hollow when tapped on the bottom. Turn out to cool on wire racks.

MAKES 2 LOAVES.

Potato-Water Bread

The foundation for this wonderful bread is the water peeled potatoes have boiled in (sometimes called potato "beer"). It has an almost magical quality—promoting the action of the yeast, giving the bread a delicious flavor, and prolonging the time before the loaf turns stale.

> *2 cups warm potato water (water that peeled potatoes have been*
>   *boiled in)*
> *5 to 5½ cups bread (high-gluten) flour*
> *1 tablespoon active dry yeast*
> *2 tablespoons granulated sugar*
> *2 tablespoons canola oil*
> *1½ teaspoons salt*

1. In a mixing bowl, combine the potato water, 2 cups of the flour, and the yeast. Beat well with a wooden spoon. Cover and let stand overnight, or up to 12 hours.

2. Add the sugar, oil, salt, and 1 cup of the flour. Beat well. Gradually add enough flour—2 to 2½ cups—to make a stiff dough. Turn out on a floured surface and knead until smooth and elastic. Turn into an oiled bowl, turning the dough once to oil the top. Cover and let rise until doubled, about 1 hour.

3. Divide the dough in half. Shape into loaves and place in well-greased 9 × 5-inch loaf pans. Cover and let rise until doubled, 45 to 60 minutes.

4. Meanwhile, preheat the oven to 375°F. Bake the loaves in the oven for 35 to 40 minutes, or until the loaves sound hollow when turned out and tapped on the bottom. Cool on wire racks.

MAKES 2 LOAVES.

Kansas Wheat Bread

Most people know that Kansas is part of the breadbasket of America, but few realize that the Mennonites who migrated to Kansas from the Ukraine contributed to that bounty by bringing their Turkey Red wheat seed with them. As families planned and packed for the long voyage to their new home, the smallest children were given the task of sorting through bags of wheat, selecting the very best kernels to be packed as seed grain for planting at their final destination.*

> 2 cups warm water
> 1 tablespoon active dry yeast
> ¼ cup vegetable oil
> ¼ cup honey or molasses
> 3 cups whole wheat flour, stone-ground preferred
> 3 cups bread (high-gluten) flour
> 1 teaspoon salt

1. In a large mixing bowl combine the warm water, yeast, oil, and honey. In another bowl, stir together the whole wheat flour and the bread flour. Add 4 cups of this flour mixture to the yeast mixture and beat well with a wooden spoon. Cover this and let stand to form a sponge, about 30 minutes.

2. Stir down the sponge. Stir in the salt. Add enough of remaining flour mixture to make a soft dough (about 1 cup). Sprinkle the remaining flour on a kneading surface. Turn the dough out onto the flour and knead gently until smooth and elastic, letting the dough pick up flour to prevent sticking. Form the dough into a ball and place in a greased or an oiled bowl. Cover and let rise until doubled, about 1 hour.

3. Punch the dough down. Divide in half. Shape into loaves and place in well-greased 9 × 5-inch pans. Cover and let rise until the loaves reach the top of the pans, 30 to 45 minutes. Meanwhile preheat the oven to 375°F.

*Voth, Norma Jost. *Mennonite Foods and Folkways from South Russia.* Intercourse, PA: Good Books, 1990.

4. Bake in the oven for 35 to 40 minutes, or until the loaves sound hollow when tapped on the bottom. Cool on wire racks.

MAKES 2 LOAVES.

Roggenbrot, or Rye Bread

I was delighted to find flour in bulk packaging in an Amish market and, thinking of a quaint little mill, inquired about its origin. The bearded shopkeeper told me with a twinkle in his eye, "It comes from a warehouse. I think it's Pillsbury." As it turns out, I prefer the somewhat finely ground Pillsbury flour for this recipe.

Some bakers bake all three loaves side by side in one large pan (about 9 × 13 inches). I prefer to bake them separately in their own individual pans, so that each loaf develops a crust on all sides.

> 2¾ cups warm water
> 1½ tablespoons active dry yeast
> 1 teaspoon granulated sugar
> ½ cup white vegetable shortening, melted
> ½ cup molasses or dark corn syrup
> 1 tablespoon salt
> 2 cups medium rye flour
> 2 cups whole wheat flour
> 5 cups bread (high-gluten) flour

1. Place 2 cups of the warm water in a large mixing bowl. Place the remaining ¾ cup water in a measuring cup. Stir the yeast and the sugar into the water in the cup. Add the shortening, molasses, and salt to the water in the bowl. When the yeast has foamed up in the cup, add it to the shortening mixture.

2. In another bowl stir the flours together, and then add 5 cups of the flour mixture to the shortening mixture. Beat well with a wooden spoon. Gradually add enough remaining flour to make a stiff dough. Turn out onto a floured surface and knead until smooth and elastic, 5 to 7 minutes. Place the dough in an oiled bowl, turning once to oil the top

of the dough. Cover bowl with plastic wrap and let rise until doubled in bulk, about 1 hour.

3. Punch the dough down and divide into 3 parts. Shape each part into a loaf and place in well-greased 9 × 5-inch loaf pans. Cover and let rise until doubled in bulk, 30 to 45 minutes. Preheat oven to 375°F. Bake until the tops are browned and the loaves sound hollow when tapped on the bottom. Turn out on wire racks to cool.

MAKES 3 LOAVES.

"Bubbat"

Since this is a favorite among the Mennonites who migrated from Russia, and since I have always seen it enclosed in quotation marks, I would guess the name is adapted from Russian. Some cooks use milk in their "bubbat," but I prefer to use only water. When a large smoked sausage is used, it is often cut into small pieces and buried between two layers of the bread dough. In this recipe, links are simply pushed into the soft dough, leaving just the tops exposed.

1½ cups warm water
1 tablespoon active dry yeast
2 tablespoons granulated sugar
3½ to 3¾ cups bread (high-gluten) flour
1 large egg
1½ teaspoons salt
6 (1 pound) link smoked sausages (I use fully cooked)

1. In a mixing bowl combine the warm water, yeast, sugar, and 2 cups of the flour. Beat well with a wooden spoon. Cover and let rest 15 minutes. Add the egg and salt and beat well. Gradually add enough remaining flour to make a stiff batter. Cover and let rise 30 minutes.

2. Transfer the dough to a greased 9 × 13-inch pan. Grease your fingers and use them to spread the dough in an even layer. Space the sausages evenly over the dough, laying them down horizontally,

and press them in as far as they will go. Cover and let rise until the dough has risen to almost cover the sausages, letting only the very tops show, about 1 hour.

3. Meanwhile, preheat the oven to 375°F. Bake the "bubbat" in the oven for 40 to 45 minutes, or until the top is well browned. Let cool slightly in pan on a wire rack and cut into serving pieces. Serve with mustard and pickles.

MAKES 6 HEARTY SERVINGS.

Plain and Simple Rolls

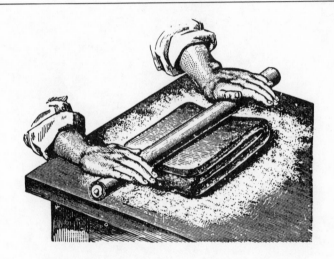

Zweiback is the stellar attraction of this chapter. Although making them may not look particularly difficult, they do require a certain knack for stacking two balls of dough to form a double-decker roll that remains upright in baking. I have devised my own methods for accomplishing this task, as you will see. It was also my great pleasure to spend a day with an experienced Mennonite baker who taught me her methods to do the same thing.

Icebox Rolls with the variations Cloverleaf Rolls and Butterhorns will supply all the dinner rolls you will ever need. Cinnamon Rolls are something you will want to make a specialty of for your breakfast pleasure.

My Own Zweiback

Zweiback means twice-baked, but these rolls are only baked once. To the Mennonite baker, twice-baked means two rolls baked at once, referring to the stacking of balls of dough to form the finished roll.

Whenever I visited my grandma Nachtigal, I headed straight for her kitchen. There she would sit me down at her oilcloth-covered table. She always fussed about, giving the impression she was annoyed that I was hungry, but I knew she was secretly pleased. Why else would she have my favorites on hand? First she poured a bowl of *moos* (fruit soup) from a pitcher she kept in her refrigerator. Then she retrieved two zweiback from a cloth-covered bowl on the counter. I ate both the soup and the rolls cold. No butter was offered or needed. Zweiback are wonderful hot, the first time around, but I still like the leftovers cold.

I have altered my grandmother's recipe, employing a simpler method of stacking the two balls of dough. I think the rolls are every bit as good as hers.

¼ *cup warm water*
1 *tablespoon active dry yeast*
1 *teaspoon plus 1 tablespoon granulated sugar*
2 *cups milk*
¼ *cup (½ stick) unsalted butter*
¼ *cup white vegetable shortening*
2 *teaspoons salt*
6 *to 7 cups unbleached all-purpose flour*
1 *teaspoon canola oil*

1. In a large bowl, combine the warm water and yeast with 1 teaspoon of the sugar. Let stand while doing the next step.

2. In a small saucepan, combine the milk, butter, shortening, salt, and the 1 tablespoon of sugar. Heat together, stirring, until the butter and shortening are melted. Let cool to lukewarm and then add to the yeast mixture. Add 4 cups of the flour and beat well with a wooden spoon. Gradually add enough remaining flour to make a soft dough.

3. Turn out on a floured surface and knead until smooth. Place the oil in a large bowl and put the dough in the bowl, turning the dough over so that the top is oiled. Cover with plastic wrap and let rise until doubled, 1 to 1½ hours. Punch the dough down, cover again, and let rise for 30 minutes.

4. Divide the dough into 3 parts. Using 2 of the parts, shape 30 golf ball–sized pieces of dough and place on well-greased baking sheets. Divide the remaining dough into 30 balls, about half the size of the first. Place one small ball on top of each large ball and immediately press one finger straight down through the center of each stack, all the way to the pan. Cover lightly with plastic wrap and let rise for 30 to 45 minutes.

5. Meanwhile, preheat the oven to 400°F. Bake the rolls for 18 to 20 minutes, or until lightly browned.

MAKES 30 ZWEIBACK.

Baking Day with Bertha Toevs

I have my own grandmother's recipe for zweiback, because my cousin Bernice watched Grandma make them, writing everything down as it happened. But I myself did not see them being made. So, when the opportunity arose for me to spend a day with Bertha Toevs of Newton, Kansas—mixing, shaping, and baking zweiback and *blechkuchen* (page 122)—I jumped at the chance. Bertha has made zweiback all her life, many of them for the Bread Basket Bakery, which she ran for years in downtown Newton. A Mennonite baker is judged on how well her zweiback stand up in baking, and I knew I would be learning from an expert.

I arrived at Bertha's at 11:00 A.M. and was told not to worry about lunch. We would eat some zweiback before the day was over. Bertha had dough ready to shape when I came in, so we set about working with that first thing. Bertha's method of shaping zweiback is called *"kneping"* (sounds like "kanepping"), and this is how it is done:

Punch the risen zweiback dough down. Take a large fistful of the dough in one hand and work it by slapping it with the other, or "spanking the baby," and pulling the sides down to shape a smooth ball-like top. Place the dough in your right hand and close your hand around the dough. Squeeze it through a circle made with your thumb and index finger. When the right size ball emerges, about 1½ inches in diameter, squeeze the dough to separate the ball from the rest. (Do not twist the dough.) Place the ball of dough on a greased or nonstick baking sheet. Repeat until 12 balls are made. (If the surface of the dough you are working with becomes rough instead of smooth, pick up another portion and start over with the process.) After the large balls are made, continue *kneping,* making slightly smaller balls of dough. Place 12 of them on a smaller baking sheet. Cover both sheets with clean cloths and allow to rise until doubled, 30 to 45 minutes.

When the balls of dough are risen, fill a small bowl with cold water. Dip a finger in the water and then use that finger to poke a hole in the center of each of the large balls of dough. Go almost, but not quite, all the way through to the baking sheet. Dip your finger into the water before poking each ball of dough. Next, pick the small balls of dough

(continued on page 102)

(continued from 101)

up, one at a time, and quickly use one finger to lightly moisten the bottom of the ball and then place it in the center of one of the large balls of dough. Do this with a slight pressure to seat the balls of dough. When all the balls have been stacked, let them stand while you preheat the oven to 400°F. When the oven is ready, turn the heat down to 350°F and place the zweiback in the oven. (Take care not to tilt the pan, lest the zweiback fall over.) Bake for 15 to 20 minutes, or until well browned. Cool on wire racks. Eat these without butter. Homemade jam is not only allowed, it is encouraged.

MAKES 36 ZWEIBACK.

We next mixed dough for a second batch. Here are the ingredients and directions:

> 2 cups whole milk, scalded
> 1 cup unsalted butter, half may be shortening, melted (Bertha
>   often uses all margarine instead)
> ½ cup granulated sugar
> 1 tablespoon salt
> 1 cup warm water
> 2 to 3 tablespoons active dry yeast (depending on how "zippy"
>   your yeast is)
> 8 to 9 cups all-purpose flour (unbleached flour can be used, but
>   do not use bread flour)

In a large bowl combine the scalded milk, butter, sugar, and salt. In a small bowl stir together the warm water and yeast. When the milk mixture has cooled to lukewarm or warm, add the yeast mixture and 3 cups of the flour. Beat this mixture with a wooden spoon until smooth and then gradually add enough additional flour to make a soft, smooth dough. Turn out on a floured surface and knead gently for about 7 minutes. Place the dough in a greased bowl, turning once to grease the top. Cover and let rise until doubled, when the *kneping* (described above) begins.

* * *

(continued on page 103)

(continued from page 102)

It was getting to be about 2:00 and I was getting a little lank, but Bertha was definitely in charge. She wasn't totally satisfied with our last batch of dough. We had used a strong (bread-type) flour that someone had given her, and the gluten content was causing too much elasticity, which in turn caused "too many" rolls to fall over during baking. (In Bertha's mind, one roll falling over is too many.) So we repeated everything again, this time with an all-purpose flour.

After our baking chores were finished, Bertha took off her apron, removed the oilcloth from her table, and replaced it with a beautifully embroidered tablecloth. She set the table with her finest china and goblets, and announced that we were to have *Faspa*.

Faspa is a late lunch (four o'clockish), usually served on Sunday afternoon. It consists of zweiback and kuchens that are left over from Saturday's baking day, along with sliced cheeses and sausage, fresh fruit, and homemade jams, pickles, and relishes. As with all good food served in a homelike atmosphere, it is a way of bringing the family together.

As we sat down to enjoy our repast, Bertha said with her characteristic smile, "There is no reason for people to have bad food at their table."

Icebox Rolls

These are biscuit-shaped rolls that are wonderfully plump—perfect for spreading with apple butter at dinnertime. I like to split, butter, and broil leftovers for an English muffin substitute at breakfast, or fill them with sandwich meats for a cold lunch at my desk.

⅓ cup plus ¼ teaspoon granulated sugar
⅓ cup white vegetable shortening
2 teaspoons salt
1½ cups milk, scalded
1 tablespoon active dry yeast
⅓ cup warm water
1 large egg
5¼ to 5½ cups unbleached all-purpose flour

1. Place the ⅓ cup sugar, shortening, and salt in a mixing bowl. Pour the hot scalded milk over these ingredients. Stir to dissolve the sugar and the shortening. Let stand until the mixture is lukewarm.

2. Meanwhile, in a small measuring cup combine the yeast, water, and the ¼ teaspoon sugar. Stir to soften the yeast. Let stand until the milk mixture has cooled. Then add the egg, the yeast mixture, and 3½ cups of the flour to the milk mixture. Stir until all the dry ingredients are moistened, then beat vigorously with a wooden spoon 50 strokes. Add the remaining flour, ½ cup at a time, being sure to mix thoroughly after each addition.

3. Transfer the dough to a greased bowl. Cover with plastic wrap and refrigerate to chill. The dough should be refrigerated for at least 6 hours, or up to as long as 3 days.

4. When ready to bake, remove the dough from the refrigerator. Punch the dough down. Toss the dough on a lightly floured surface until no longer sticky. Divide in half. Roll one half to a 6 × 12-inch rectangle (the dough should be about ½ inch thick). Cut 8 rolls with a floured 3-inch biscuit cutter and place the cut pieces on a greased or nonstick baking sheet. Reroll scraps and cut two additional rolls. Repeat with the remaining dough, or rechill the second half for later use. Cover with plastic wrap and let rise until doubled, 1 to 1½ hours.

5. Meanwhile, preheat the oven to 350°F. When the rolls have risen, bake in the preheated oven for about 15 minutes, or until browned. Serve warm.

MAKES 20 ROLLS.

Cloverleaf Rolls

There's no need to have a multitude of recipes for dinner rolls, if you have a basic recipe that can be used several ways. Such is the case with my Icebox Rolls. They are easily shaped into these Cloverleaf Rolls and the Butterhorns that follow.

Follow the recipe for Icebox Rolls. When ready to bake, grease 24 4-ounce muffin cups. Divide the dough in half and shape each half into 12 balls. Divide each ball into 3 parts and again shape into balls. Place three of the small balls into each muffin cup. Cover the muffin tins with plastic wrap, and let dough rise until doubled, 1 to 1½ hours. Preheat oven to 375°F. Bake for 12 to 15 minutes, or until lightly browned.

MAKES 24 ROLLS.

Butterhorns

Follow the recipe for Icebox Rolls. When ready to bake, divide the dough into 3 parts. Roll each part on a lightly floured surface into a 12-inch circle. Spread the circle with about 2 tablespoons melted butter. Cut (as for pie) into 8 equal wedge-shaped pieces. Starting at the wide end, roll up toward the point. Place point-side down on a greased or nonstick baking sheet. Curve the ends slightly. Repeat with the remaing two parts of dough. Cover the rolls with plastic wrap and let rise until doubled, 1 to 1½ hours. Preheat oven to 375°F. Bake for 12 to 15 minutes, or until lightly browned.

MAKES 24 ROLLS.

Cinnamon Rolls

These cinnamon rolls use the raisin-filled dough from Rich Raisin Bread. The brown sugar–cinnamon filling and the vanilla-flavored glaze make them irresistible.

ROLLS
Rich Raisin Bread dough (page 91)
2 tablespoons unsalted butter, softened
½ cup light brown sugar, firmly packed
2 teaspoons ground cinnamon

GLAZE

1½ cups powdered sugar

1 teaspoon vanilla extract

2 to 4 tablespoons hot water

1. Prepare the rolls: Grease two 8 × 8 × 2-inch baking pans. Prepare the dough for Rich Raisin Bread. After the first rising, punch the dough down and divide in half. Working with one half of the dough, roll or press out on a lightly floured surface to a 9-inch square. Spread the dough with half the butter. Mix the brown sugar and cinnamon together, then sprinkle half the mixture on top of the butter. (Caution: the sugar almost doubles in volume in the mixing. Be sure to use ½ of the sugar mixture on each half of the dough.) Press lightly to firm. Roll up to form a log. Cut into 9 equal slices. Place the slices, cut-side down in one of the baking pans (3 across, 3 down). Repeat with the remaining dough. Cover and let rise until almost doubled in bulk, 30 to 45 minutes.

2. Meanwhile, preheat the oven to 350°F. Bake the pans of rolls in the oven for 25 to 30 minutes, or until browned. Turn out on wire racks to cool, right-side up.

3. Prepare the glaze: In a small mixing bowl, stir together the powdered sugar and vanilla with enough hot water to make the mixture spoonable. Spoon the glaze over the tops of the rolls. Serve warm.

MAKES 18 CINNAMON ROLLS.

Quick Bakery Breads
and Coffee Cakes

The charm of quick breads is that they *are* quick and easy. Finger Biscuits and Breakfast Biscuits are a snap to make to help start your day. Old-fashioned Corn Bread and Cornmeal Muffins can be whipped up for noon or nighttime. For something sweet, try Apple Butter Muffins, Crumb Cake Muffins, Buttermilk Crumb Cake, Streusel Blueberry Coffee Cake, Cinnamon Flop, or Plum Kuchen. The Wafers are a delightful cracker that can be eaten alone or used in the traditional way with creamed chicken. There are two coffee cakes in this chapter that use yeast, but neither of them is difficult to execute—Fruit *Plautz* and *Blechkuchen*.

Finger Biscuits, or *Schnetke*

My father had seven older brothers, all of them farmers. While we were living in Hawaii, we didn't have the opportunity to see them.

Automobiles were precious commodities on the islands, as their sales prices included high shipping costs; used cars were sold and resold rather than being traded for new. In response to this my dad came up with a grand scheme. The family would travel by ship to the West Coast of the mainland. There we would board a train for Detroit where we would buy a new car at the factory. Then we would drive to San Francisco where we would board a ship for the trip back. The car would be loaded into the ship's hold for our use when we returned home. The journey would also give Dad a chance to see his brothers.

We executed Dad's dream, and what an adventure it was. On the trip back across the country we stopped at our relatives' to visit, and I became acquainted with aunts, uncles, and cousins I had never seen. Many of the cousins were almost the same ages as my brother, sister, and I and were so close to us in appearance that we found ourselves aligning with our almost-twins for fun and mischief.

Everywhere we stopped there was wonderful food: fried chicken or rabbit from backyard hutches, the meat sweet and succulent in its freshness; fruits filled with the full ripeness of the sun; and vegetables bursting with the goodness of well-tended care. But the most memorable part of the meal was always the home-baked cakes, pies, breads, and biscuits. I particularly cherished these tender little finger biscuits.

Waste not, want not. The dough for these biscuits is shaped into a rectangle. The dough is buttered, folded, and cut into finger shapes instead of circles. No need to worry about what to do with the scraps.

2¼ cups bleached all-purpose flour
1 tablespoon baking powder
½ teaspoon salt
1 teaspoon sugar
½ cup white vegetable shortening
¾ cup milk
2 tablespoons unsalted butter, melted

1. Preheat the oven to 450°F.

2. In a mixing bowl whisk together the flour, baking powder, salt, and sugar. Cut in the shortening until mixture is the texture of coarse cornmeal. Add the milk and stir with a fork just until the dough comes together.

3. Turn out on a lightly floured surface and roll into a 12 × 8-inch rectangle, about ¼-inch thick. Spread with the melted butter. Fold the dough in half lengthwise, forming a 6 × 8-inch rectangle. Press lightly to seal. Cut in half to make two 3 × 8-inch rectangles. Cut each of these rectangles into eight 1 × 3-inch fingers. Place them on an ungreased baking sheet and bake in the preheated oven for 10 to 15 minutes, or until the biscuits are risen and golden brown. Cool slightly on the baking sheet. Serve warm with honey butter or apple butter.

MAKES 16 BISCUITS.

Breakfast Biscuits

This recipe uses the shortcut of homemade self-rising flour. I sometimes get even further ahead of the game by cutting the shortening into the flour before trundling off to bed. In the morning all I need to do is stir in the buttermilk and bake. Milk can be substituted for buttermilk if you decrease the amount to 1¼ cups.

> *3 cups Homemade Self-rising Flour (page 127)*
> *½ cup white vegetable shortening*
> *1⅓ cups buttermilk*

1. Preheat the oven to 450°F.

2. Measure the Homemade Self-rising Flour into a mixing bowl. Cut in the shortening with a pastry blender or two table knives. Add the

Menno-Hof

Of all of the Mennonite-Amish museums, visitors centers, and educational displays I have visited, the Menno-Hof Mennonite-Amish Visitors Center in Shipshewana, Indiana, is the best. In a handsome cluster of buildings, you will find multimedia presentations that depict the history of the Anabaptist movement and interpret the faith and life of the Mennonites and the Amish. Although part of the tour requires a guide, many of the displays are self-directed. The buildings themselves were constructed with the techniques that the Amish use when erecting a barn for one of their neighbors. Rough-sawn beams are fastened together with only knee braces and wooden pegs, and the entire structure was finished in six days by a crew using only handheld tools.

At the end of the tour, you will find a sales area stocked with wonderful Amish and Mennonite cookbooks. The center is a joint project of four Anabaptist groups: Beachy-Amish, Conservative, General Conference Mennonite, and Mennonite Church.

buttermilk and mix with a fork just until all the dry ingredients have been moistened.

3. Transfer the dough to a lightly floured surface and toss until no longer sticky. Press and fold the dough lightly and gently 3 to 4 times to distribute the moisture evenly. Do not work the dough roughly or knead it as you would a yeast mixture. Roll or press out to ½-inch thickness. Cut with a 3-inch round biscuit cutter and place on an ungreased baking sheet. Re-form scraps, roll, and cut additional biscuits, as needed. Bake in the oven for 10 to 15 minutes, or until the biscuits are risen and golden brown. Cool slightly on baking sheet. Serve warm with butter and homemade jams and jellies.

MAKES 12 LARGE BISCUITS.

Wafers

These wonderful crackers are like little squares of baked pie pastry. Traditionally served with creamed or stewed chicken, they can be scattered on top of a serving or placed on the plate first, the chicken ladled over the top. They also make good snacks, so if you plan to have them with your chicken for supper, you'd better store them out of sight.

> *2 cups unbleached all-purpose flour*
> *½ teaspoon salt*
> *½ teaspoon baking powder*
> *1 teaspoon granulated sugar*
> *½ cup white vegetable shortening*
> *1 large egg*
> *3 to 6 tablespoons milk*

1. Place the oven rack in the upper third of the oven. Preheat the oven to 350°F.

2. Mix the flour, salt, baking powder, and sugar together. Cut in the shortening until the mixture is the texture of coarse cornmeal. In a measuring cup, use a fork to mix the egg with 3 tablespoons of the

milk. Add to the flour mixture and stir with a fork. Add additional milk, 1 tablespoon at a time, stirring with the fork, until the dough holds together like pie dough.

3. Divide the dough in half and roll out, one part at a time, on a lightly floured surface, to a thickness slightly less than ⅛ inch. Cut into 1-inch squares and transfer to ungreased baking sheets. Prick each wafer 2 or 3 times with a fork. Bake one sheet at a time in the oven for 10 minutes, or until the wafers are lightly browned. Shake the wafers loose and slide them off onto a clean counter to cool. (They're too small to cool on most wire racks.) If some wafers brown before the others, remove them and return the remaining wafers to the oven to bake a little longer.

MAKES 16 DOZEN WAFERS.

Old-fashioned Corn Bread

Buttermilk and cornmeal, baked in a seasoned cast-iron skillet, make a memorable corn bread. I would like to be able to tell you there is a pan you can successfully substitute for the skillet, but I can't. If you don't have a 10-inch cast-iron skillet, enjoy the cornmeal muffins that follow instead.

¼ cup white vegetable shortening
1½ cups yellow cornmeal
¾ cup bleached all-purpose flour
1 teaspoon baking soda
½ teaspoon salt
¼ cup granulated sugar
2 large eggs
1¼ cups buttermilk

1. Preheat the oven to 425°F. Place the shortening in a 10-inch cast-iron skillet and place in the oven just until the shortening is melted, 1 to 3 minutes. Remove the skillet from the oven and tilt to coat the sides with the melted shortening.

2. In a mixing bowl, stir together the cornmeal, flour, baking soda, salt, and sugar. In a small bowl stir together the eggs and buttermilk and add them to the dry ingredients. Pour in the melted shortening from the skillet. Stir the mixture together until all ingredients are moistened. Pour the batter into the skillet and bake in the oven for 20 to 25 minutes, or until the top springs back when lightly touched in the center. Cut into wedges and serve warm, directly from the skillet.

MAKES 8 TO 9 SERVINGS.

Cornmeal Muffins

There is nothing better than homemade corn muffins, and these are especially good. They have enough cornmeal to give them a good "corny" flavor, and just enough sugar to make them pleasingly sweet. I use supermarket degerminated cornmeal, just like my mother did.

1¼ cups yellow cornmeal
¾ cup bleached all-purpose flour
1 tablespoon baking powder
½ teaspoon salt
3 tablespoons granulated sugar
1 large egg (use the largest from a dozen sized large)
1 cup milk
3 tablespoons canola oil

1. Preheat the oven to 425°F. Line with paper liners or grease 12 4-ounce muffin cups.

2. In a mixing bowl stir together the cornmeal, flour, baking powder, salt, and sugar. In a smaller bowl stir together the egg, milk, and oil. Add the liquid ingredients to the dry ingredients and stir together just until all dry ingredients are moistened.

3. Spoon the batter into the muffin cups, filling ¾ full. Bake in the oven for 15 to 20 minutes, or until risen and lightly browned. Cool slightly on a wire rack. Serve warm.

MAKES 12 MUFFINS.

Apple Butter Muffins

Velvety smooth, spicy-flavored apple butter is a staple in the Amish-Mennonite home. A jar is always on the table, ready to spread on hot rolls or toast. It's used in the kitchen too, baked into breads, cakes, pies, and muffins like these. Despite their cakelike texture, they are a snap to make. Serve them for a lunch or brunch buffet. Offer sweet butter and apple butter for spreads.

1½ cups bleached all-purpose flour
½ cup granulated sugar
½ teaspoon salt
½ teaspoon baking powder
½ teaspoon baking soda
½ teaspoon ground cinnamon
¼ teaspoon ground nutmeg
½ cup (1 stick) unsalted butter, melted
1 large egg
¾ cup apple butter

1. Preheat the oven to 400°F. Grease 12 4-ounce muffin cups or use nonstick.

2. In a large bowl whisk together the flour, sugar, salt, baking powder, baking soda, cinnamon, and nutmeg. Melt the butter in a small saucepan and set aside to cool slightly.

3. In a mixing bowl, beat the egg with a wooden spoon until smooth. Stir in the apple butter. Slowly pour in the melted butter, stirring constantly. Add the liquid ingredients to the dry ingredients, stirring just until the mixture is smooth.

4. Spoon into the muffin cups, filling ⅔ full. Bake in the preheated oven for 15 to 18 minutes, or until the tops of the muffins spring back when lightly touched in the center. They should not brown. Cool on wire racks. Serve slightly warm.

MAKES 12 MUFFINS.

Crumb Cake Muffins

Of all the Amish-Mennonite recipes I have eaten, researched, and made, crumb cakes have to be my favorites. I wanted to adapt the idea to a muffin format, and after many unsuccessful attempts, triumphed with this one.

2 cups bleached all-purpose flour
½ cup granulated sugar
½ cup light brown sugar, firmly packed
½ cup (1 stick) unsalted butter, slightly softened
½ teaspoon salt
½ teaspoon baking powder
½ teaspoon baking soda
1 large egg
⅔ cup buttermilk
1 teaspoon vanilla extract

1. Preheat the oven to 400°F. Line 12 4-ounce muffin cups with paper liners.

2. In a bowl mix the flour and sugars together. Cut in the butter until the mixture is reduced to fine crumbs. Lightly spoon out ¾ cup of the crumbs and reserve.

3. Mix the salt, baking powder, and baking soda with the remaining crumbs. Add the egg, buttermilk, and vanilla and mix until all ingredients are moistened. Some small lumps may remain.

4. Fill the muffin cups ¾ full. Sprinkle about 1 tablespoon of the reserved crumb topping over each muffin. Bake in the oven for about 20 minutes, or until well risen and lightly browned. Remove to cool on wire racks. Serve at room temperature.

MAKES 12 MUFFINS.

Buttermilk Crumb Cake

This is, no doubt, the grandmother of all crumb cake recipes.

2½ cups bleached all-purpose flour
1 cup granulated sugar
1 cup light brown sugar, firmly packed
½ teaspoon salt
1 teaspoon baking powder
1 teaspoon baking soda
½ cup (1 stick) unsalted butter, softened
1 cup buttermilk
1 large egg
1 teaspoon vanilla extract

1. Preheat the oven to 350°F. Grease a 9 × 13-inch baking pan.

2. In a large mixing bowl, stir the flour, sugars, salt, baking powder, and baking soda together. Cut in the butter to make fine crumbs. Lightly spoon out 1 cup of crumbs for topping.

3. Add the buttermilk, egg, and vanilla to the remaining crumbs and mix until only small, grainy lumps remain. Spread in the prepared pan. Sprinkle the reserved crumbs on top. Bake in the preheated oven for 30 minutes, or until a wooden pick inserted in the center comes out clean. Cool in pan on a wire rack.

MAKES 12 TO 16 SERVINGS.

Streusel Blueberry Coffee Cake

Every Amish-Mennonite baker has her favorite streusel coffee cake. This is mine. The size is perfect for today's smaller family; and it's not too rich, making it appropriate for breakfast any day of the week. Although blueberries have a tendency to sink when added to a batter, I counter that by laying down a thin layer of the batter in the pan before folding the blueberries into the remaining mixture.

STREUSEL
⅓ cup bleached all-purpose flour
¼ cup granulated sugar
¼ cup light brown sugar, firmly packed
½ teaspoon ground cinnamon
3 tablespoons unsalted butter

CAKE
1 large egg
⅔ cup granulated sugar
⅓ cup vegetable oil
1 teaspoon vanilla extract
1½ cups bleached all-purpose flour
2 teaspoons baking powder
½ teaspoon salt
½ cup milk
1½ cups fresh blueberries

1. Preheat the oven to 350°F. Grease an 8 × 8 × 2-inch pan.

2. Prepare the streusel: In a food processor, mix the ⅓ cup flour, ¼ cup granulated sugar, the brown sugar, cinnamon, and butter to make fine crumbs. (Alternately, stir together the dry ingredients, then cut in the butter to make the crumbs.) Set aside.

3. Prepare the cake: In a mixing bowl, beat the egg and the ⅔ cup granulated sugar with a wooden spoon until thick and lemon colored. Add the oil and beat again. Mix in the vanilla. In another bowl sift or whisk together the 1½ cups flour, baking powder, and salt, and then

add alternately to the egg batter with the milk (3 parts dry ingredients, 2 parts milk).

4. Spread about ¼ of the batter in the pan. Fold the blueberries into the remaining batter. Spoon into the pan. Sprinkle the reserved streusel mixture over the top. Bake in the oven for 25 to 30 minutes, or until the top is lightly browned and a wooden pick inserted in the center comes out clean. Cool in pan on wire rack. Serve warm.

MAKES 9 SERVINGS.

Cinnamon Flop

There cannot be a more quaint name for a recipe than Cinnamon Flop. It must have flopped in the eyes of the first cook who made it, earning its name. Nonetheless, it survived that trial and has become a standard in Amish-Mennonite cookery. It's easy to whip up and so good, I like to bake it for a quick breakfast coffee cake.

> *2 cups bleached all-purpose flour*
> *½ cup granulated sugar*
> *1 tablespoon baking powder*
> *½ teaspoon salt*
> *6 tablespoons unsalted butter*
> *1 cup milk*
> *¾ cup light brown sugar, firmly packed*
> *1 teaspoon ground cinnamon*

1. Preheat the oven to 350°F. Grease an 8 × 8 × 2-inch baking pan.

2. In a bowl mix together the flour, sugar, baking powder, and salt. Rub in 2 tablespoons of the butter to make crumbs. Add the milk and stir just until the dry ingredients are moistened. Do not overmix.

3. Spread in the prepared baking pan. Sprinkle with the brown sugar, then the cinnamon. Cut the remaining butter into 16 chunks and push into the topping, spacing evenly (4 rows across, 4 rows down).

119

4. Bake in the preheated oven for 30 to 35 minutes, or until lightly browned. Cool in pan on a wire rack. Serve warm.

MAKES 9 TO 12 SERVINGS.

Plum Kuchen

Kuchen means "cake," and a Plum Kuchen is an easy-to-make fruit coffee cake.

TOPPING
¼ cup bleached all-purpose flour
¼ cup granulated sugar
2 tablespoons unsalted butter, slightly softened

CAKE
1½ cups bleached all-purpose flour
¾ cup granulated sugar
2 teaspoons baking powder
¼ teaspoon salt
1 large egg
½ cup milk
¼ cup canola oil
4 medium red plums, pitted and sliced

1. Preheat the oven to 375°F. Grease and flour a 9 × 13-inch baking pan.

2. Prepare the topping: In a small bowl, stir the ¼ cup flour and ¼ cup sugar together. Cut in the butter to make crumbs. Reserve.

3. Prepare the cake: In a medium bowl, sift or whisk together the 1½ cups flour, ¾ cup sugar, baking powder, and salt. In a small container whisk the egg, milk, and oil together. Add the egg mixture to the dry ingredients and mix just until the dry ingredients are moistened. It is OK to have some small lumps. Spread the batter in the pan. Arrange the plum slices in 3 long rows on top of the batter. Sprinkle the crumbs over the plums. Bake in the oven for 30 to 35 minutes, or until a wooden

pick inserted in the center comes out clean. Cool in pan on a wire rack. Serve warm.

MAKES 12 SERVINGS.

Fruit Coffee Cakes, or *Plautz*

Plaut means "flat or low," and for this cake a thin layer of yeast dough is covered with a layer of sliced fresh fruit. A crumb topping is sprinkled over all, and the cake is baked in a moderate oven. If a Mennonite cook is making zweiback, she might use part of that dough for the base of her *plautz*. The dough need not rise after the *plautz* are assembled, but if you don't have room in the oven for all three at once, cover one with plastic wrap and let it rise while the other two bake.

PLAUTZ
1 teaspoon active dry yeast
¾ cup warm water
1 tablespoon granulated sugar
2¼ cups unbleached all-purpose flour
½ teaspoon salt
3 tablespoons unsalted butter, softened
4½ cups sliced fresh fruit, such as peaches, pears, plums,
   nectarines, or apples

CRUMBS
1 cup bleached all-purpose flour
1 cup granulated sugar
½ teaspoon ground cinnamon
4 tablespoons unsalted butter, softened

1. Prepare the *plautz*: In a medium-size bowl, soften the yeast in the warm water with the 1 tablespoon sugar. Let stand 5 minutes. Add 1 cup of the unbleached flour and beat well. Stir in the salt and the 3 tablespoons butter; add 1 cup additional flour and mix well. Add the remaining ¼ cup flour, 1 tablespoon at a time, mixing well after each

addition, until the dough forms a ball that cleans the bowl. Cover with plastic wrap and let rise for 45 minutes.

2. Preheat the oven to 350°F. Lightly grease 3 9-inch pie pans.

3. Punch the dough down. Divide into 3 parts. On a lightly floured surface, roll each part to a circle to fit a 9-inch pie pan. Transfer the dough to the pans and gently stretch the dough to come up the sides of the pans. Fill each pan with ⅓ of the cut-up fruit, arranging the slices in concentric circles.

4. Prepare the crumbs: Mix the 1 cup bleached all-purpose flour, 1 cup sugar, and cinnamon together. Rub the 4 tablespoons butter in with your fingers to make crumbs. Sprinkle the crumbs over the fruit, dividing evenly among the pans. Without further rising, bake in the oven for 30 to 35 minutes, or until the fruit is tender and the crust is browned. Cut in wedges and serve warm.

MAKES 3 *PLAUTZ*, SERVING 12 TO 18.

Blechkuchen

This recipe was demonstrated for me during my visit to the Newton, Kansas, kitchen of Bertha Toevs. It is a flat coffee cake that is delicious for Sunday breakfast. The raisins can be either dark or golden. When sprinkling the sugar on the top of the kuchen, Bertha, who never measures, says to sprinkle as much sugar as you think you need, then sprinkle some more.

KUCHEN
1 cup milk, scalded and cooled to warm
1½ tablespoons active dry yeast
½ cup granulated sugar
¾ teaspoon salt
1 large egg
6 tablespoons unsalted butter, melted
3 to 3¼ cups unbleached all-purpose flour

1 cup raisins, floured with 1 tablespoon unbleached all-purpose flour

TOPPING
2 tablespoons unsalted butter, melted
4 to 6 tablespoons granulated sugar, according to your taste

1. Prepare the kuchen: Pour the milk into a mixing bowl and sprinkle the yeast over it to soften. Add the ½ cup sugar, salt, egg, and 6 tablespoons butter. Add three cups flour and beat well with a wooden spoon. Stir in the floured raisins. Add additional flour, if needed to make a soft, spoonable dough. Cover and let rise until doubled, about 1 hour.

2. Spoon the dough into a greased 10 × 15 × 1-inch pan and spread evenly over the bottom and partway up the sides with your hands or a spatula.

3. Prepare the topping: Drizzle the dough with the 2 tablespoons melted butter. Sprinkle with 4 to 6 tablespoons sugar. Cover with waxed paper and let rise until almost doubled, 30 to 45 minutes. Meanwhile, preheat the oven to 350°F. Bake the kuchen in the oven for 15 to 20 minutes, or until golden brown. Cool in pan on a wire rack. Serve slightly warm or at room temperature.

MAKES 18 SERVINGS.

Standard Preparations

There are a few do-ahead recipes that come in handy if you like to keep a steady volume of Amish-Mennonite baked goods coming from your busy kitchen. The first is Homemade Self-rising Flour for making breakfast biscuits. The Crumb Topping can be used on coffee cakes, fruit pies, muffins, and more. The Cinnamon Sugar can be sprinkled on cookies, pie crusts, breads, and rolls. In addition, I have given here the double- and single-crust pastry recipes for pies, rather than repeat them in every recipe where they are needed.

Homemade Self-rising Flour

Breakfast Biscuits (page 111) are a snap when the flour, salt, and leavening are premixed.

> *12 cups bleached all-purpose flour*
> *¼ cup baking powder*
> *1 tablespoon baking soda*
> *1 tablespoon salt*

1. Combine all the ingredients in a very large bowl. Mix thoroughly with your hands by repeatedly plunging them into the mixture, fingers down, and then bringing the bottom part of the mixture to the surface with your palms up.

2. When mixed, transfer to a container with a tight-fitting lid and store in a cool, dry place.

MAKES ABOUT 12 CUPS SELF-RISING FLOUR.

Crumb Topping

This all-purpose topping is good for impromptu use on muffins and fruit pie fillings. Once, when preparing a family meal with a Mennonite theme, I found that time was running away from me. My planned Dutch Apple Pie was beginning to look impossible. After a quick trip to the nearby grocer, I filled a prepared pie shell with canned apple pie filling, finished it off with my trusty Crumb Topping, and popped it in the oven. I arranged my beautiful unused apples as a centerpiece, and my family devoured the pie.

> *1½ cups bleached all-purpose flour*
> *1 cup light brown sugar, firmly packed*
> *½ cup (1 stick) unsalted butter*

1. Mix the flour and brown sugar together. Cut in the butter to form crumbs.

2. Store in a tightly covered container in a cool, dry place. If you lack a cool pantry, store in the refrigerator.

MAKES ABOUT 3 CUPS CRUMBS.

Cinnamon Sugar

My mother always had a container of this sugar in her cupboard, ready to sprinkle on leftover scraps of pastry when she made pies. She baked these scraps on a flat sheet before the pies went into the oven, while I eagerly awaited my treat (see Pie Crust Cookies, p. 74).

> *1 cup granulated sugar*
> *4 teaspoons ground cinnamon*

1. In a bowl mix the sugar with the cinnamon.

2. Store in a large salt or sugar shaker (a container with a screw-on perforated lid).

MAKES ABOUT 1 CUP.

Pastry for a Double-Crust Pie

2 cups bleached all-purpose flour
1 teaspoon salt
¾ cup white vegetable shortening
4 to 6 tablespoons cool water

1. In a small mixing bowl stir together the flour and salt. With a pastry blender, cut in the shortening until only small lumps remain. Add the water, 1 tablespoon at a time, stirring with a fork after each addition. Add only enough water to make the dough come together.

2. Gently pat the dough into a ball, cover with plastic wrap, and refrigerate to chill while preparing your pie filling. Roll out and shape as directed in recipe.

MAKES ENOUGH PASTRY FOR A 9-INCH DOUBLE-CRUST PIE.

Pastry for a Single-Crust Pie

1⅓ cups bleached all-purpose flour
½ teaspoon salt
½ cup white vegetable shortening
3 to 4 tablespoons cool water

1. In a small mixing bowl stir together the flour and salt. With a pastry blender, cut in the shortening until only small lumps remain. Add the water, 1 tablespoon at a time, stirring with a fork after each addition. Add only enough water to make the dough come together.

2. Gently pat the dough into a ball, cover with plastic wrap, and refrigerate to chill while preparing the pie filling. Roll out and shape as directed in recipe.

MAKES ENOUGH PASTRY FOR A 9-INCH PIE SHELL.

Bibliography

For further reading about Amish–Mennonite history, culture, and foods, I suggest the following books.

Fisher, Sara E., and Rachel K. Stahl. *The Amish School* (Intercourse, PA: Good Books, 1986).

Good, Merle, and Phyllis Pellman Good. *20 Most Asked Questions About the Amish and Mennonites* (Lancaster, PA: Good Books, 1979).

Good, Phyllis Pellman. *Cooking and Memories* (Lancaster, PA: Good Books, 1983).

Hostetler, John A. *Amish Roots: A Treasury of History, Wisdom, and Lore* (Baltimore and London: Johns Hopkins University Press, 1989).

Kraybill, Donald B. *The Puzzles of Amish Life* (Intercourse, PA: Good Books, 1990).

Nolt, Steven M. *A History of the Amish* (Intercourse, PA: Good Books, 1992).

Pellman, Rachel T., and Joanne Ranck. *Quilts Among the Plain People* (Lancaster, PA: Good Books, 1981).

Ruth, John L. *A Quiet and Peaceable Life* (Intercourse, PA: Good Books, 1985).

Scott, Stephen. *Amish Houses & Barns* (Intercourse, PA: Good Books, 1992).

———. *The Amish Wedding: And Other Special Occasions of the Old Order Communities* (Intercourse, PA: Good Books, 1988).

———. *Plain Buggies: Amish, Mennonite, and Brethren Horse-Drawn Transportation* (Lancaster, PA: Good Books, 1981).

———. *Why Do They Dress That Way?* (Intercourse, PA: Good Books, 1986).

Scott, Stephen, and Kenneth Pellman. *Living Without Electricity* (Intercourse, PA: Good Books, 1990).

Voth, Norma Jost. *Mennonite Foods & Folkways from South Russia: Volume I* (Intercourse, PA: Good Books, 1990).

———. *Mennonite Foods & Folkways from South Russia: Volume II* (Intercourse, PA: Good Books, 1991).

Index

135

About the Author

Marilyn Moore is a descendant of the "Russian" Mennonites who moved across Europe to Ukraine at the invitation of Catherine the Great. When their exemption from military service was threatened, they traveled back across Europe, boarded ships for New York City, and eventually settled in Oklahoma and Kansas.

Moore is a member of the International Association of Culinary Professionals and is a Certified Culinary Professional. She is the author of eight books, including) *The Wooden Spoon Book of Old Family Recipes* (previously titled *Meat and Potatoes and Other Comfort Foods from the Wooden Spoon Kitchen*) and *The Wooden Spoon Dessert Book*. She is currently teaching baking classes on America Online. She lives in Scottsdale, Arizona, with her husband, Joe, and her calico cat, Demi.